GROWING KI

GROWING
KNOWING
JESUS

IAN COWIE

THE SAINT ANDREW PRESS
EDINBURGH

First published 1978 by
THE SAINT ANDREW PRESS
121 George Street, Edinburgh

© Ian Cowie

ISBN 0 7152 0385 1

Printed and bound in Great Britain by
Bell & Bain Ltd.

CONTENTS

CONTENTS

PREFACE

This book is for beginners,
> although, who knows, sermon-hardened church folk may get something out of it too!

It is for the person who
> has fragments of a picture of Jesus lying around in his mind, but has never tried to complete the jig-saw.

It is for the person who
> long ago rejected the childish idea of Jesus, but who is now wondering if there's not something in it after all.

This study of Jesus' life began as a course for adults joining the church, beginning in October and ending at Easter, and that is why it takes the form it does, although it does not need to be read that way.

You may wonder why in this book there are only four days in the week! My experience is that not many people can manage seven days, each with a reading to be done. People get behind and then give up. But if you are taking it a little bit each night, then you will probably manage four nights a week.

It is a good idea to have one or two friends doing the same readings so that you can discuss it together, with or without a minister or some 'expert' in the background to refer to for extra help.

One man's views—that is all that I can give. No one person can give the whole answer for everybody, but I offer you what has come to me as I have followed Jesus. In some ways it may help, but it will never be the whole answer. I know that many people I know and respect would disagree with a lot that I have written, but it would be boring if I tried to give every possible interpretation of each verse! I offer you a series of pointers to Jesus, and pointers are *meant* to be left behind. If this book has pointed to HIM, then it has served its purpose, even if you decide that in some ways I am wrong. It is Jesus himself who is the 'Way, the Truth and the Life'; words can only take you so far. I hope you will grow to know Jesus for yourself as you read on.

A BIBLE?

Just a word or two about the Bible first, although if you are familiar with it, you can skip the next page or two. If you are setting out on the spiritual voyage ahead equipped only with a small, musty book in antique English, then I guess that you will not get far. After all, we want to get as clear a picture as we can of Jesus. We want to get the feel of what he said, and see a vivid picture of him in action.

Our information about Jesus came to us written in Greek, because it was the language of the market place and of educated conversation. In the original, his words come over with a fresh, earthy feel about then, and we do not get the feel of them if we read them in 'churchy' language. In some cases the writers actually pass on to us the words Jesus used in the dialect he spoke, Aramaic. They are homely words, not least the word 'Abba', which is what a child called a father at home, 'Dad' might get the feel of that word best. When Jesus addressed God as 'Abba' people were shocked, or thought it wonderful, depending on how they looked at it.

Of course we value the master-piece we call the 'Authorized Version', which is still regarded as 'The Bible' by many English-speaking people. It has its place. But modern translations which catch the hard-hitting, earthy quality of the Gospels also have a place. So we will look at some of the modern versions which are available. But no matter which one you decide to work on, remember that a good, well-bound Bible with big print will help you, and it is worth your while to take some trouble to get yourself properly equipped for your 'search'.

VARIOUS VERSIONS

The Authorized Version came out in 1611 after King James had gathered the best scholars he could find, and set them to work on the Greek and Hebrew manuscripts which had been discovered in the previous century.

A BIBLE?

The Revised Version came out in 1881–85, because scholars had found documents that were not known to King James's men, some mistakes had come to light, and some of the old English had become too outrageous for modern ears, but by and large it left the work much the same to the casual hearer.

The American Standard Revised Version came out later, tidying it up still further, and this was then gone over by Roman Catholic scholars, which resulted in a recent version acceptable to both sides called *The Common Bible*.

The New English Bible was the result of work by British scholars who went back to even older documents, and who had the advantage of all sorts of recent archaeological discoveries to help them understand what phrases meant. It came out in full in 1970.

The Jerusalem Bible was the parallel work by Roman Catholics, who up till then had depended on the Latin Bible, called *The Vulgate*.

Good News For Modern Man came out in recent years because many felt that modern people, who are not used to reading, needed something even simpler.

The Living Bible is set out to appeal to modern, conservative American young folk, and is free with additions and alterations to make it more acceptable. It is a paraphrase rather than a translation.

Many individuals, such as Dr Moffatt and J. B. Phillips, have made their own translations of the whole or of parts.

While many parts of the Authorized Version (AV) are so beautiful that they can never be replaced, many other parts of the Bible only come to life when you read them in fresh, modern words. Most of us work basically on the AV but have our favourite modern version as well.

EXPLORING YOUR BIBLE

If you take up your Bible, and look through it, you will find that about two-thirds of the way through there is a division. The first part is called *The Old Testament*. It is basically the Bible of the Jews. Roughly speaking it was the Bible known to Jesus, and is the Bible used by Jews today. It was written in Hebrew, and the last bits in it were written centuries before Jesus came.

The last third of the Bible is called *The New Testament*. It is made up of writings in Greek: not the classical Greek of great literature but the common Greek which was spoken all over the Mediterranean world at the time of Jesus. It is a collection of all sorts of writings by people who were close to Jesus, and all the information about Jesus is to be found in this part of the Bible. Our Jewish friends, of course, do not have this as part of their Bible. You may choose a New Testament by itself—and it would be quite possible to read this book along with a New Testament on its own—but it would be better to have a whole Bible.

Some people find it hard to distinguish between the New Testament and a new translation. But if you have read this far, you will know that King James's men translated both the Old and New Testaments into their seventeenth-century English, and modern scholars translate both Testaments into modern English. So you can have a new translation of the New Testament, or an old translation of it!

Most Bibles have an index, showing you where to find the different books. Some printers have separate indexes for the two sections, and even start numbering again at page one of the New Testament. A little bit of exploring will soon sort out these issues.

Introduction

Our first week's readings are arranged to help you find your way around. Nearly all our information about Jesus is to be found in the four Gospels, and by the year AD 100 each of these was circulating separately under the name of its supposed author, and there were others too. By the year 200 the four we know had been bound together, and were recognized as being authoritative.

If you are working from a complete Bible, then you will find them about two-thirds of the way through, at the beginning of The New Testament, but if you are working from a New Testament, then, of course, they are at the beginning. We find our way to a particular passage by a system of numbered chapters and verses. This is a fairly recent idea, going back only to 1551, but it is very useful. For instance, when you see 'Mark 1:1-5' you look up St Mark's Gospel, find chapter 1 and then read the first five verses, as shown in the small numbers down one side of the print.

It is a good idea to have your Bibles, say an Authorized Version and a New English (AV and NEB) with this book handy beside your fire or bed, where you can reach them easily at a regular time each day. You look to see which passage is suggested, say 'Mark 1:1-5'. You read it in the AV and in the NEB; then you see what the notes in this book say about it. The really important thing is what happens next: you think about what this says to you. Reading the Bible is not like reading other books. You read, and then you try to digest that small bit. Ideally you should turn that into a prayer, saying to God something like: 'Help me to live that out today.' Your Bible passage should become the beginning of a conversation with the Lord, and the hope is that as you read on, that conversation will become more lively.

Mark 1:1–5

A very old book tells us that St Mark was secretary to St Peter, Jesus' leading disciple, or 'apprentice' as we would say. In the year AD 64 the Roman Emperor Nero had St Peter crucified, and so his secretary wrote out the stories which Peter used to tell. In a real way, we might call this St Peter's Gospel, and we get a very short, clear, down to earth view of Jesus through this Gospel.

It begins by reminding us that Jesus came at the end of a two thousand-year preparation, as recorded in The Old Testament. For centuries one Jewish prophet after another had looked forward to *Somebody* who was coming. They had various ideas as to what that Somebody was to be like.

Then John the Baptist, a cousin of Jesus, appeared saying that the Somebody was here. His hard-hitting sermons drew the crowds, and he dipped (that is the meaning of 'baptized') people in the river as a sign that they were sorry for where they had gone wrong, and were ready to make a fresh start, in preparation for the great day when the Somebody would come into the open.

If they had had newspapers in those days, reading them would have given you the impression that the world was in just as big a mess as ours is today. In fact in many ways the violence, immorality and corruption of the Roman Empire was worse than ours. Yet through it all, God was working out His Purposes. Nobody at the time would have dreamed that *the* important thing happening in the world was the arrival of a joiner from a remote village at a revivalist meeting beside an unimpressive river. Perhaps we forget that God is still working out His Purposes in our world today, and that what hits the headlines is very seldom what is really significant.

Now lay this book aside, and have a few minutes thinking quietly about what all this says to you, and try to say something to God about it, in your own words.

Matthew 1:1 and 18

Matthew's Gospel comes first, but it was probably not written first, since it seems to include whole passages quoting from Mark.

It begins by reminding us that Jesus was part of a family whose roots go back 2,000 years to Abraham. If you know your Bible, you will know that many of these names are familiar to us, and not a few family tragedies are involved; for instance see the story of Ruth in the Old Testament, referred to in verse 5. When she was widowed she little dreamed that her personal tragedy would become part of the greatest story in the world!

Then, at verse 18 we find: 'This is the story of the birth of the Messiah.' That word 'Messiah' is a Hebrew word meaning 'anointed'. We are more familiar with the Greek version of it: 'Christos', from which we get 'Christ'. It is another word for 'king', for in those days kings were anointed rather than crowned. So the word 'Christ' is a title, not a surname.

Jesus' surname would have been Bar-Joseph, 'bar' being like 'mac' in Scotland, meaning 'son of'. As we will see later, Jesus carefully skirted round this title of Messiah during his life, but the early Christians were in no doubt that he was the long-awaited king whose kingdom should be world-wide and everlasting, and they called him Jesus, the Messiah. His own name, Jesus, is in Hebrew Yeshua, with the accent on the U. It was a common boy's name, and about 1200 years earlier there had been a great bearer of that name, though we usually spell it Joshua. It is a name which means God-Rescuer.

Nobody sensible doubts that Jesus bar-Joseph of Nazareth was a real man. The question is: Was he or was he not the fulfilment of the promises of the Old Testament, the King of Kings and Lords of Lords? That is for you to decide as you read this book. In your few minutes of quietness now, ask God to help you to sort out the truth.

Luke 1:1–4

This is a very different opening. Luke was a Greek doctor, a friend of St Paul. You could say that as St Mark's Gospel might be called St Peter's, so St Luke's might be called St Paul's. Paul had been executed at the same time as Peter, but all his letters had been circulating in the church for some years, so they are all earlier than the Gospels.

Luke explains that in his travels with Paul, as he tells us in Acts, he had found many attempts to tell the story of Jesus, and we can see that St Mark's Gospel was one of them. So he explains that he had sifted them carefully and put them together. As was the custom in those days, he addressed his writings to an important person, in this case Theophilus, but we do not know who he was.

The way this Gospel opens reminds us that it was written by a highly intelligent, educated man, who had worked hard at the story to get it right. It is quite wrong to imagine that the Gospels were written by superstitious peasants, and if you examine St Luke's Gospel carefully, you will find it the work of a highly intelligent, sensitive man. Another misconception to dispose of is the idea that the Gospels were written generations after Jesus. This idea was common earlier in this century. But research has shown that the first three were written probably by the 70s at the latest, or perhaps even earlier. As I write this, it is in the late 70s of this century, and things which happened in the 30s are easy to remember, or to find eye-witnesses for.

Generations of scholars have been sifting out the Jesus-stories. There are always radicals trying to say that they are all nonsense, and conservatives trying to maintain the literal, verbal truth of every word, and there are many shades in between. You read for yourself, never mind the extremists and the cranks, and do not be afraid to question and to seek answers. The Truth is not afraid of honest seekers.

John 1: 1–14

St John was one of Jesus' first followers, and his closest friend. We think that his Gospel was written down about AD 90 by his helper, also called John. It seems to take for granted that you have read the others, and does not retell what they have said. It is very different from the other three, and there is a lot of discussion about this.

Mark began by seeing Jesus in the setting of the Prophets, and Matthew began by seeing him in the context of the family tree. John began by seeing him in the setting of the whole universe. It is a very deep passage, and you can spend a life-time learning from it. What he is saying is that there is purpose, meaning, behind the whole of creation, and that purpose was embodied in Jesus.

This approach helps us because it reminds us that we are not arguing with science as such. Some scientists are Christian and most are not, just as some grocers are Christian and most are not. Scientists have shown us a logical universe, and the word which is translated in most of our Bibles as 'The Word' is in Greek: 'Logos', from which the word 'logic' comes. So when John says that there is one underlying Logos, he says something to which scientists can say 'amen'. Then he goes on to say that this Logos was 'embodied', made flesh, in Jesus. That is going further, and many who would say 'amen' to the first bit would draw the line there. The Christian sees in Jesus the clue to the whole mystery of life, the Logos behind the universe.

'One damn thing after another' is how modern people express the feeling that life is meaningless. It is this meaningless-ness that drives people to drugs and to drink; it is the spiritual disease of our day. We maintain that as you come to know Jesus, you begin to see meaning and purpose in life. Jesus is not 'kid's stuff'; he is the mystery behind the universe, the centre on which all the lines of truth converge. This is John's message.

5

Introduction

Modern discoveries, such as the Dead Sea Scrolls, have helped us to know a lot more about the times in which Jesus lived than any previous generation knew since those who actually remembered them.

The TV news has made us only too familiar with the geography of Palestine, but let us check it over. Nazareth is a hill village in the northern highlands, and from it the road winds down to Lake Gennesaret, or the Sea of Galilee as we call it. In those days its fishing potential had led to a build-up of the fishing industry, and its milder climate had led many non-Israelis settling there. The Jordan flowed from it to the Dead Sea in the south, and from there you climb up dry, arid mountains until you come to Jerusalem on its hill-top. Nazareth to Jerusalem would be about the same journey as going from Edinburgh to Carlisle.

At that time the Romans were occupying Palestine and the 'Free Israel' movement, called 'The Zealots', was very strong. We know from the history books and records that riots and risings were common, and the Jews understood the Bible to mean that Somebody was going to come and free them from the Romans. Time and again men would lead armed revolts claiming to be the Messiah, only to be crushed brutally. On one occasion we know of, the Romans crucified 2,000 people at once.

This, then, was the world-stage upon which Jesus of Nazareth stepped out into the limelight. It is not 'once upon a time', but a strangely familiar world, about which we know a lot. Many other famous people lived then, and were writing books which you can still read today.

Mark 6:1–6

This story actually comes later on in Jesus' ministry, but what the neighbours say gives us almost our only clue to his background before he became a public figure, apart from the stories of his birth.

Look at the clues they give us:

Verse 3. *The Carpenter:* he was a tradesman and, if he had lived today, would have dressed in dungarees.

> *The Son of Mary:* what had happened to Joseph? Presumably he must have been dead for some time. This would have left Jesus, as first-born, in charge of a family of four boys and at least two girls.

As we have seen, they were hard days, with starvation always around the corner. The riots and risings left a trail of hunger and disease. The threat of slavery was always over their heads, and Rome's army and secret police were everywhere. So, to keep a widowed mother and six other youngsters would have been a hard job. There was no social security, no sickness benefit. It was work or starve.

So Jesus did not arrive with a pat religion worked out in some temple-school. He had hammered it out the hard way. He was not 'holy' in the usual sense of the word, and people were surprised when he began preaching. As they would say in Scotland: 'I kent his faither.' Perhaps we have to revise our picture of what he would have looked like: a gnarled Israeli joiner, used to working from dawn to dusk to support the family, a man who had *survived* in a far harder world than we would care to face.

But why is there so little about this part of his life? Perhaps it is that there is little to tell. His first step was to become 'one of us'; just one of the nameless, toiling masses.

Think over quietly: what is your picture of Jesus?

Luke 3:1–17

We take a closer look at the figure mentioned in Week 1, Day 1: John the Baptist. Luke begins by giving us the actual year. In those days that is how they referred to years, for, naturally, they could hardly use BC and AD! We would say 'In AD 26'. This reminds us that this is not fairy-story stuff, but dated and placed firmly in reality.

John was giving them strong stuff, and there are times when plain talking is needed. We need to be faced with our petty dishonesties, our greed, our excuses and our impurities. We cannot begin to put things right until we have faced what is wrong. There is no treatment until the disease has been diagnosed. So Jesus' fore-runner prepared the way by making people face God's Law of Goodness. The way Jesus acted when he did come into the open was not what John had expected, and John was later puzzled by Jesus. John did his job, but he was not infallible.

Later on Jesus reminded people that he had not come to water down what John and the prophets had taught about goodness, in fact he was going to require a higher standard of goodness altogether. John came saying 'You have *GOT* to be good.' Jesus came to make it possible for us to be truly good.

A modern Christian summed goodness up in Four Absolutes: Absolute Love, Absolute Purity, Absolute Honesty, Absolute Unselfishness. John would have approved of that, but it terrifies us. But as we come to know Jesus, new heights of goodness become possible, and we rise to these new heights, not out of fear, as John suggested, but out of love.

In the meantime, take the Four Absolutes, and test yourself by them, quite ruthlessly. Face the symptoms of the disease we call 'sin', and face that you could never rise to the heights of goodness. Then you are ready to discover the reality of Jesus.

Mark 1:9–11

Down from his hill-village came Jesus, just as one of the crowd. The call to national repentance, the summons to be ready for some new purpose that God had in mind, led him, with many others, down into the water. In that moment he had an experience. It is always hard to explain such an experience, and when he tried later to tell Peter and the rest about it, it must have been almost impossible to find words. Sunday School pictures of a light and a dove may put us off too!

Whatever it was that happened, it left him sure that he was the one for whom Israel had been waiting. We often discuss how much Jesus knew before this, and some people are sure that he knew all along that he was The One. Others are sure that he did not, and of course you can quote the Bible to prove anything! If it had been important for us to know, it would have been made plainer. What we do know is that up to this point his behaviour had not led anybody to think of him as something special, whereas after this, he acted as if he had a quite unique part to play in human history. Some people, then as now, thought him mad. The test of a religious experience is in its results: 'The proof of the pudding is in the eating.'

To some of us too there come moments of insight, when we suddenly *know* that God loves us and has a purpose for us. But this is not an every-day experience. Such a moment may or may not come our way, it is no use seeking it. We get on with earning a living, caring for the family, and responding to what seems to be God's Word for us, then, if it comes, well and good. People can become unbalanced looking for 'conversion experiences' and the like. Each of us, as we follow Jesus, can come to know with a deep sureness, that *we* too are God's beloved children in whom he delights. Be still now, and let The Word of God say those words to you personally: 'You are my beloved child.'

Luke 4:1–13

Jesus now knew that he was The One. But there was no ready-made scheme to follow. How could he, a village joiner, fulfil the promises in the Bible of setting up a world-wide kingdom? Look how many others had set out in great faith and had failed! He knew what everybody was expecting, but were they right? No wonder he rushed off into the desert to work it out. ('Forty days' is a Jewish phrase meaning 'a long time'.) People who fast get into a state where they see things very vividly, in dream form, and later when Jesus told the disciples about this experience they would know that. His hunger was his first temptation: to use his powers to feed himself. Don't we fall for that one without even noticing that it is there? Use what skill you have to feed yourself, and then see what's left over to help others. But Jesus right through his life refused to use his power for his own benefit.

He was then tempted with a vision of that world kingdom promised in the Bible. It is tempting to think that evil *is* the strongest force in the world, and perhaps you do have to come to terms with it in order to gain power, *then* you can do good. Hitler, Stalin, Napoleon and others fell for this one.

Then he was tempted to think that a display of power would do the trick. But he knew that he had to take the long, hard road of service to win men's love, and not try to frighten them into obedience.

So he worked through the alternatives, but though he was 'in the clear' for a bit, we notice that it was only for the time being; he was tempted to take the wrong path right up to the end. 'He was tempted as we are', wrote a later writer. Do we realize what a struggle he had? To realize this brings him a lot closer to us. When we are not sure what to do, when Bible verses seem to point in opposite directions, we can turn to him as one who has been through it. Maybe your temptations are a bit different, but the basic battle is the same.

Introduction

This week takes us on to the beginning of Jesus' public work. We see him beginning to build up a fellowship with which to work, a fellowship which will eventually include you and me. In a sense, this is where we come in.

By now I hope you are beginning to get into the way of things, seeing that reading the Bible is different from reading an instruction manual or a novel. For the Christian, Bible-reading and prayer are interlinked and one cannot flourish without the other. 'Prayer' is not saying words in some high-sounding language. We have seen already that God reveals Himself in a working man, and that is because He wants us to talk to Him 'man to man' ('person to person' does not have the same ring to it!)

In our Bible-readings we try to 'tune in' to Jesus, by reading the passage. Having got on to his wavelength, so to speak, we then bring before him the practical concerns of our lives. It may be that the reading has pointed us to something we have overlooked in our lives, or to somebody who needs our prayers. It may just lift up our hearts so that we want to sing for joy, or we may just want to be still and let God's Peace enfold us. There are all sorts of ways of responding to a passage.

Some people like to pray out loud, some like to 'think' to Him. God knows our thoughts, so there is no need for spoken words, although there are times when we *do* feel the need to give voice to our prayers, either because we are so happy, or because we are in such anguish.

Perhaps the simplest form of prayer is built on the basis of 'Thank you, Sorry, Please'. We look back and see what there was during the day to say 'Thank you' for. Then we look back to see what there was to say 'Sorry' about, and finally we think of what we need to ask Him for, for instance 'Please bless so-and-so.'

John 1:35–51

Leaving the desert, Jesus meets up with two of John's followers. One fetches his brother, the other, we guess, was John himself, for you'll notice that he even remembers the time of day!

On their way north they meet somebody else from their hometown, and he contacts a friend of his, Nathaniel. That pattern of meetings all looks so casual. Jesus has not started a publicity campaign or anything, yet people are drawn in. Things are beginning to take shape among friends, neighbours, relatives and so on. God works through the ordinary, the down to earth, and that is the message of Jesus in itself. That conversation with Nathaniel is puzzling, but if he had been meditating while he sat under the fig-tree, perhaps about Jacob's vision of the ladder between earth and heaven, then the whole thing makes sense.

You will notice that at this early stage they use the word Messiah quite glibly. As yet they are still thinking that it means what they have been brought up to think it means. Later on they will think twice about using it.

So 'the church' begins quite simply, as a bunch of working men trudge northwards.

With us too, it is through all sorts of little coincidences, chance meetings and everyday happenings that we begin to find that we are being linked up with Jesus. As with them, many of the ideas we begin with have to be altered as we go along. People often expect God to break into their lives with visions, angels, miracles, etc., and they are disappointed. All the time He is at work through little commonplace things.

And you, as you read this?
Who knows what He has in mind for you?
You don't, that's certain!
God knows.

Mark 1:14–15

We have no idea how much time elapsed between the end of that walk northwards and the beginning of Jesus' work in earnest as recorded here. Presumably they all went back to their jobs, and who knows whether they saw each other occasionally or not? Then John the Baptist was arrested, and thrown into prison for attacking the royal morals. That must have been a depressing time for good Israelis, so it must have seemed odd when Jesus began to proclaim the good news that the long-awaited Kingdom of God was upon them! It certainly did not look like it!

They had been praying for this Kingdom for centuries, and were expecting it to be ushered in with a gigantic upheaval, with a glorious King leading the Jews to victory, establishing them as the master-race ruling the world. No wonder they were puzzled when Jesus said it had arrived, and there was no call to arms, not a sword in sight. What on earth did he mean, then?

As we thought yesterday, we often miss God because we are looking for Him in the wrong places, and the Jews of Jesus' time were like that. Their fixed ideas about religion blinded them to the new reality breaking through.

Our day too, is a time when conventionally religious folk are depressed. Yet some of us feel that history is repeating itself, and that this is a time when Jesus is breaking through to new things, and that we are involved, even though we only have the slightest grasp of what it all amounts to.

> Something big is 'on the go'
> and we are being called to take part in it.
> That is what we do know.
> So we must follow, and leave the rest to Him.

Mark 1:16–20

Now comes the call to get going in earnest. They have had time to talk about it with each other, but there always comes the time when Jesus ceases to be a subject for discussion and you either follow, or you don't. To miss that moment is to miss life itself.

We gather from later in the story that their boats were still there in the background, and that they went back to fishing from time to time. It would seem that Peter's home became Jesus' headquarters in Bethsaida—the fishing quarter of Capernaum—so their homes remained there too. But their lives from now on were to be about following Jesus, and these other things became secondary. Notice one thing, though. It seems to have been in the rather cosmopolitan town of Capernaum that Jesus made his headquarters, rather than in the 'Holy City'. Near this town was the crossing of the trade routes which linked Europe, Asia and Africa. It was the sort of city that strict Jews looked on with suspicion, and it was here that Jesus settled, insofar as he settled anywhere.

We also note that he chose *working* men from *this area* to be his workers, not 'holy men', not the professionally trained religious leaders. They were men whose training was in working together out on the lake with its squalls and its dangers; men who knew how to make ends meet selling fish in the market. These were the men he called and began to train.

The prophets in the Old Testament had often rammed it home that God is not confined to the 'God-box', a nice pigeon-hole marked 'Religion'. He is concerned with the whole of life. They protested that God was more interested in fair dealing in the market place than in temple rituals. Now Jesus acted it out, taking his place with working men in the workaday world.

What does that say about your work? Your home? Your training?

Mark 1:21–35

This reading gives us a picture of one memorable day, their first Sabbath together. Jesus led his men into action, but the enemy was not the Roman soldiers, but human misery and evil.

In the Jewish synagogue any adult Israeli might be invited to read from the Bible and expound upon it. This usually amounted to giving quotations from what leading authorities in the past had said about the text. Jesus just spoke out on what the Bible meant on his own authority. They were quite taken aback.

Then we have this case of the demoniac. The traditional way of dealing with 'possession' was to call upon the names of good superhuman powers (angels), until you found one whose authority was higher than that of the 'demon' on the bad side. It was an elaborate ritual, but Jesus just cut through all that. He ordered the demon out on his own authority. By their way of thinking, only God Himself could be assumed to have authority over any demon, and His Name was so holy, that you had to be very careful about invoking it. So when Jesus took it for granted that he had *that* authority, do you see why they were shaken, yet again?

After that awe-inspiring scene in the synagogue, we have the happy scene in Simon's home, with his mother-in-law. It is good to remember that the disciples had mothers-in-law!

Verse 35 reminds us of the secret of Jesus' power: prayer. Alone with the Father, he absorbed into his body the power which was later to pour out in healing. Prayer when you feel like it, or in emergencies is one thing, but what counts is the long term build-up of a relationship with God, so that His Love can flow through you. If you think you can do it all yourself provided you try hard enough, then you are sadly mistaken. These times of reading your Bible and turning your thoughts to Jesus are a beginning.

Introduction

This week we look at four incidents in which Jesus meets people with unusual results. Two of them are later to play an important part in the story. But remember that what we have in the Gospels is only 'the recorded highlights', as they say on TV. The story has been condensed, and it is left to us to imagine what might have been the whole encounter.

That brings us on to think for a moment of why these Gospels were written. They were brought out for the benefit of countless little groups of new converts, meeting in houses, often secretly, sharing bread and wine in Jesus' Name, and trying to live out the Christian life in the midst of the corruption of the cities of the Roman Empire. We know from Paul's letter to the Corinthian group that their sharing of bread and wine was a real meal, not just a ritual. In fact those who arrived early were eating and drinking too much, while those who arrived later, the slaves and those who had to work late, were left hungry.

And still today, these Gospels are best shared. They make most sense when two or three gather in a house week by week to share insights, and maybe a 'cuppa'. Bread and wine tend to make people feel strange, for it's not as natural for us as it was for them to share bread and wine.

If you are sharing this, and it is worth trying to do so, beware of one nasty modern habit: our tendency to talk more readily about what we disagree with, than about what we agree with. Keep the talk centred round what 'Light' each has received. Get each person to express his insights and then deal with two things: 1. Disagreements: By all means explore them for a bit, but remember that the solution may be found a few weeks later so don't waste time trying to get all-round agreement right away. 2. Questions: Make a note of what points of information you need, and try local ministers or libraries.

John 3: 1–17

This man Nicodemus appears in the story later when, as one of the Council, he disagrees with the death sentence on Jesus, and takes part in the Lord's burial, when 'the twelve' had all run for it. So it is interesting to watch his first approach, at night, secretly.

He must have been a very wise, learned man, and so we can see why he would have been puzzled. He would have been expecting some information or teaching to add to his vast store, instead Jesus tells him that he must be born again, starting all over again from scratch.

People who are full of self-confidence, sure that they know nearly all the answers, will never understand this. But those who have hit rock-bottom, those who have come to the end of their tether, have found that there *is* a power, a spirit, that can remake human life when given the chance.

This 'Spirit' (the Hebrew word means 'Breath' and 'Wind' as well as 'Spirit', which makes it hard for translators) makes you aware of dimensions you had never known before. You do not become aware of the Kingdom of God by learning or by self-improvement, or even by becoming a VIP in the church. It comes through being born again; becoming a little child all over again.

Verses 16–17 are some of the best known in the Bible, but are they Jesus' or are they John's words? They did not have inverted commas in those days, so we are not sure where Jesus' words stop. They emphasize that if any man ends up in darkness it is the result of *his* choice, not God's. God's only concern is to rescue us, not to condemn us. Man *is* in danger of darkness, that is why Jesus' mission was urgent. But if *He* is literally 'dying to save us', why should anybody be lost? But, of course, Love cannot force itself on anybody. So just be glad that the Light has come for you.

Mark 1:40–45

To get the hang of this story you must know that leprosy
has always been thought of as a special sign of the anger of
the gods, all over the world. People banned a leper
because they felt that if their gods were as angry as that
with the poor wretch, then to have anything to do with
him might incur the god's anger too.

Notice that in the NEB, and other modern versions, it
says that Jesus was *indignant*, whereas the AV says 'he had
pity'. That is because scholars have found that the most
reliable old documents *do* say 'angry'.

Now let us put all that together. This leper thinks of
himself as condemned, accused by God, and so he cries: 'If
it is your will. . . .' And Jesus is angry. Not at the man, but
at the idea that His Father would *want* any poor soul to
suffer from this revolting disease. It is a libel on God. So
Jesus reached out his hand and touched the man. Imagine
what that would have meant; probably nobody had
touched him for years. For one thing, Jesus was breaking
the laws of the Bible about leprosy in touching a leper
(see Leviticus 13).

Then he echoes the man's words 'Of course "I will". Be
clean.' Jesus was not concerned to grub around trying to
find out what the poor man had done to deserve this. His
only concern was to heal/save (the same word in Greek),
as we read yesterday. This was a revolutionary attitude to
illness, and many people today have still not caught up
with it, and one still hears people saying: 'What have I
done to deserve this?'

Why the secrecy in verse 43? If people just regard you
as a source of cheap, easy cures, then they can miss what is
really being said, as we find today. Publicity can ruin a
healing ministry, getting things out of proportion. Verse 45
backs up our experience today. Physical healing *is* a part
of the Gospel, but only a part.

Mark 2:1–12

Many houses in the Mediterranean area are built around a courtyard, and the natural place for Jesus to sit while speaking to a big crowd, would be in the shady corner under a light bamboo thatch, the sort of corner where the householder would sit in the evenings. The flat roof would make access easy. This 'scenery' makes it easier to have a realistic picture of what happened, than if you are thinking of one of our houses.

This story provides a contrast with the one about the leper. There, Jesus had angrily dismissed the idea that the man had done anything to deserve it, whereas here he deals with the lad's guilt first. (The word he uses is 'lad', suggesting a young man.) A psychiatrist would tell you that it is possible for a person to be paralysed by a sense of guilt, and that no treatment would get that person on his feet until the guilt was dealt with. Once it had been dealt with, the person could walk. In this case it is the *person* who has created the 'darkness' of illness for himself, not God, and this goes back to what we saw in John 3:16–17. Jesus' only concern was to heal/save. What a modern specialist would have taken months to do, Jesus does in minutes, because he speaks with the authority of God.

His riddle in verse 9 is simple: If you say 'You're forgiven', nobody can tell if you are really forgiven or not, but if you say 'On your feet!' and the person is still paralysed, you will look stupid. But of course, they were right, only God can forgive sins. It is only the wounded party who can say: 'I forgive you.' Later Jesus was to show, on the cross, that *he* is the wounded party, and therefore he has the right to forgive. He assumed the authority to forgive sins as he assumed authority to expound the Bible and to cast out demons in a way they felt was blasphemous. No wonder they said: 'Who is he?'

But to many today Jesus would say: 'Stop tying yourself in knots with guilt. You are forgiven. Get up and live.'

Does this speak to you?

Mark 2:13–17

This is a story about one of the 'publicani'. (Not a publican as we mean it.) The Romans were too clever to do their own dirty work of collecting taxes. They would sell this 'privilege' to some local man. He would then collect taxes and customs duty on the understanding that he could charge extra, and get rich on the rake-off. He was regarded as a traitor by his fellow-countrymen, as well as being unpopular.

The Jews expected the Christ to rid them of such scum, not to invite one into his fellowship! He even went to a dinner party with him and his friends, who would have been a pretty shady lot, probably. The Jews felt that eating with somebody meant saying 'We belong together'. They might have accepted it if Jesus had preached to these sinners; eating with them was to identify with them, and that was disgraceful. Such a dinner would normally take place in the type of courtyard we thought of yesterday, and it would be quite visible from the street, for in the east these dinners are public occasions for a village. So even people who had been interested and friendly up till then, would have found themselves in a very difficult position when Jesus went in through that gate to 'eat with sinners'. To follow him in there would mean identifying yourself with people that no God-fearing man would have anything to do with. What a predicament!

If Jesus came to your district, where would you expect to find him? Somebody once said: 'The Church is not a museum of saints, it is a school for sinners.' What do you make of that? An old favourite hymn says: 'Shun evil companions...', and we *have* seen people dragged down by bad company. Obviously there are very great dangers here, and false romanticism can lead us astray. In the light of our readings this week, think deeply about John 3:17: 'Not to judge, but to save.'

Introduction

This week we are going to read of how Jesus began to run into opposition. In the usual 'fairy-story' version of Jesus, it is hard to see why anybody should have wanted to get rid of him. So let us try to see why people took him seriously enough to crucify him.

It is a good time to look at this for our own benefit too. Those who begin to follow Jesus seriously soon begin to run into opposition too. People often think that being a Christian should bring 'good luck', but if that is what they are after, they should not be following Jesus. 'Good luck' may feature in the horoscopes, but not in the Gospels. The fact is that we must expect to run up against opposition, even in the places in which we had expected to find encouragement, just as Jesus found opposition among the religious people of his day. It is always painful to find oneself regarded as a threat or a crank by people you thought were serving the same God, but if this is your experience, do not worry, for Jesus and all his best followers have been in the same boat.

Following Jesus means a life of struggle. The point is that we know it is a worthwhile struggle for the good of all. Life is a struggle anyway, a struggle to survive which is always lost in the end. Only when we throw in our lot with him do we enter the struggle which ends in life, not only for ourselves, but for all, in the long run.

c

Mark 2:18–20

In the east people go in a lot for fasting: it is a sign of a truly holy man. It is thought that fasting earns merit, and it certainly produces weird visions, as we noted earlier. Most religious teachers taught their followers systems of fasting and purification.

So do you see why people were puzzled when Jesus and his friends seemed to eat and drink normally? They even went to parties with doubtful characters. That was not what was expected of a holy man.

Even today many people tend to think that if you are to be truly Christian you will be a miserable sort of person who never does anything enjoyable. The idea seems to be that Christians think that if you make yourself miserable enough on earth, there will be a reward in heaven.

So Jesus explains that there was no need for his followers to fast. Fasting is supposed to bring you nearer to God, but they were near God, just doing the ordinary things when they were with him. There was no need for religious exercises when you walked with Jesus. The long-faced Christian is as out of place as a miserable wedding guest.

Jesus foresaw times when following him would involve suffering, but while he was there with them, they should enjoy it. When the Kikuyu Christians were being slaughtered by the Mau-Mau they were discussing whether they should wear crosses as an open sign of defiance, when an old elder said: 'We have no need of them. The joy on our faces is enough sign that we follow Jesus.'

Being a holy man, a person utterly dedicated to God, does not mean becoming a religious weirdie, then. It means doing the ordinary things, but doing them with joy because you share the experience with *him*. They might sneer at Jesus because he was not 'holy' enough by their way of thinking, but his way is true holiness, and that word originally meant the same as 'wholeness'. So we are called to be 'holy', *his* way.

Mark 2:21–22

Was Jesus remembering the scene at home, when his mother wove and patched the children's clothes? She would never take cloth off her loom and patch an old jacket with that. At the first shower it would shrink and make the tear worse. When she made wine from their vine, she would not use last year's skins, which were by then all hardened. She would pick wine skins with 'give' in them, so that when the fermentation started, they could stand the strain.

People were becoming disillusioned with Jesus because he was not doing what religious leaders were meant to do. Healing and hobnobbing with 'sinners' was not bringing Israel back to the religion of their fathers. He was not standing up against the immorality and the foreign influences that were undermining the nation. He was not getting people back to church, as we would say. Then, as now, people wanted the old religion hotted up a bit. They expected better sermons to do the trick. Patch it up with more new hymns, or by reviving old ones! But, like the old wineskins, they are set in last year's shape. They want to sit where they have always sat, do what they have always done, only with plenty of new people round them, so long as the new people do not disturb the 'old faithfuls'.

All over the world people are feeling that new wine of the Spirit is being poured out, and people are finding new ways of following Jesus. The result of reading these notes may not be that you become a regular church-goer of the usual type; it may lead you into finding new patterns altogether. People who love the old wine, which itself was new once, and who find the old jacket comfortable, can get very angry with those who will not fit in. Every new movement finds this. So Jesus found the good church folk of his day turning against him. Think carefully about your local situation in the light of this. Remember that Jesus did not give up, neither should we.

23

Mark 2:23–28

Keeping the Sabbath holy, one of the Ten Commandments (see Exodus 20), was at the very heart of Jewish religion. It was this that marked the Jews off from other nations. It was a point of national pride. For Jews, then and now, the Sabbath is from 6.00 p.m. Friday till 6.00 p.m. Saturday. It was originally meant so that everybody would have a day's rest, even the slaves and the animals. In a world which took slavery for granted this was a wonderful rule. The idea that God was interested in conditions of employment and the rights of the workers was a great step forward when Moses received it about 1400 BC.

But over the following centuries men had turned the Sabbath into something which had become a burden, not a blessing. They had worked it out legalistically, and concluded, for instance, that you might *save* life on the Sabbath, but healing was 'work', so it was wrong to heal. Therefore if a man was bleeding to death, you could staunch the flow, but you must not put on a dressing. We may think it quite ridiculous, but ask the older generation about Sabbath Observance in Scotland; no Sunday papers, but you could read the Monday papers which had been printed on Sunday!

So it is that what begins as a blessing turns sour, and becomes a burden. Therefore Jesus swept many of these rules aside. 'The Sabbath was made for man', it was meant to help us, he said. He, and his friends, did things on the Sabbath which broke the rules which the religious authorities had worked out, so they became very angry, for their authority was being challenged. They were quite sure that they were right, and that the Bible backed them up. They saw Jesus as a wicked Sabbath-breaker, who was undermining their national religious institutions.

Could it be that some of our national and religious conventions need looking at again, not to water them down to popular standards, but to allow better ideas of goodness to flourish?

Mark 3: 1–6

We have seen previously how Jesus assumed authority:

> over demons,
> to interpret the Bible in a new way,
> to pronounce the forgiveness of sins,
> to heal the sick,
> to break the rules about the Sabbath.
> to call men to become *his* followers.

Here, in this story, we see all these summed up in one incident, and the result was that both the super-nationalist pharisees and the supporters of the puppet regime got together for once, united in their realization that this man was a menace. If a man assumed authority such as this, an authority which none of them would dare to claim, they must either claim that he is mad, or they must accept his authority. But to envisage what accepting that authority might mean was terrifying. So parties who were normally daggers-drawn, literally, united to get rid of this usurper.

It looks as if they had deliberately set up this trap for Jesus. An old tradition says that the man was a stone-mason. In those days an injured man got no compensation or insurance, and if he could not work, he just had to beg. Now these religious leaders who were meant to be representing God's concerns were using this man's misery as a pawn in their own game. This is the second time we have read that Jesus was angry, and once more it is over the question of the attitude to human suffering on the part of religious teachers.

Try to imagine how Jesus appeared in the eyes of these god-fearing, patriotic leaders. To what extent is the call to be a follower of Jesus a call to be a revolutionary of a sort? If you are connected with a congregation already, to what extent does its worship and activity represent Jesus' blazing compassion for the lost, the sick, the suffering?

Introduction

One of the outstanding things about Jesus is his way of getting points across by simple stories. At least, they *look* simple. Yet people find new depth in them in every generation; you read them, and think: 'I get the point', but years later you see something else which had never struck you before. So don't be taken in by the simplicity on the surface; these stories are worth deep study.

We call this type of story *a parable*, and there are two things worth noting about these parables:

1. Most of them convey truth about God that was quite revolutionary in Jesus' day. In fact many who call themselves Christian have not caught up with them yet; perhaps none of us has!

2. Even from the point of view of story-telling, these parables are masterpieces, perhaps especially the Parable of the Prodigal Son which we look at this week. A master-mind is needed to produce masterpieces, so there is no doubt that there really was a master-mind somewhere about the time we associate with Jesus, and that he left behind him a fund of stories which have been challenging people to re-think their ideas about God and about life ever since. If the author was not Jesus of Nazareth, who was he? It is easier to accept that Jesus was the story-teller. Non-Christians have to accept that this man is one of the Great Men of the world, but Christians go further and maintain that in him we meet with God.

Christian and non-Christian alike can pay tribute to the *man*, Jesus.

Luke 15:1–7

In every age men build temples, churches, shrines and so on, and they form religions. They also form systems of law to govern society. But equally, in every age there are some who just don't fit. The religion does not ring any bells for them. Their own desires and weaknesses lead them into trouble with the law. The religious, law-abiding folk tend to look down their noses at these others. They get a kick out of condemning them and relish sermons condemning sinners. Sometimes their condemnation leads to torture, prison and death, all done 'in the Name of God'.

But how *does* God feel about sinners? This parable suggests that we have to do a lot of re-thinking. Perhaps, as you read this, you know that you are one of the people who have gone wrong, one of 'the lost sheep'. Perhaps the religious people you know have given you the impression that God is just itching to fling you into a never-ending torture-chamber. Or perhaps you are sure that you are safely within the fold and you wonder why more people don't come to church. From the safety of the fold, you look down on the people outside, and wait for your reward. Either way this parable is a bomb-shell.

If you have a hymn-book with 'There were ninety and nine' in it, look it up and think it over. It was written by a girl who had heard that her 'black sheep of the family' brothers had died in exile. Don't just say 'Yes, very nice' and leave it. Have a good long think about what you think the word 'God' means, and see if it fits in with what Jesus is saying here.

Luke 15:11–32

A lot of people are annoyed by this story, and of course Jesus meant them to be. They think that by their goodness they have earned a reward, and are bitter that it has not turned out like that . . . like the elder brother. Jesus was constantly trying to overturn the idea that God works on a 'reward and punishment' basis, with scales of 'good luck' as rewards for good deeds, and of 'bad luck' for bad deeds. We have already seen that he challenged it by his attitude to illness, now he attacks it by this story.

The key to the story lies in verse 31: 'My boy, you are always with me', said the father, and that is what Our Father offers us: His Company. 'Everything I have is yours', he said, and we know from earlier in the story that this was true. The older son could have had a party any time he wanted to, it was all his! But his negative attitude led him to nurse a sense of injustice. He had missed the point as badly as the 'prodigal son'.

Isn't it time we took a fresh look at how God's love watches out for us, yearns for us, waiting for us to come to ourselves, and see that our place in His Home is there waiting for us, however dirty or awkward we may have become? Psalm 73 has something to say about this.

Goodness which looks for a reward is just disguised selfishness. Real goodness is concerned for the good of others and looks for any possible chance of reconciliation, even with the worst. It reflects God's only concern: that all His Children should find their way home eventually.

Luke 18:9–14

The Pharisee: the super-religious nationalist, self-confident, sure that if there were more people like him the world would be a better place.

The Publican: tax-gatherer for the Roman occupation army, hated as a traitor to his country, outlawed from his religion.

Even the worst men have their moments of truth, when they weep for what they are. If at that moment there is somebody near them, who can listen and understand, then they may find their way to a new life. If there is nobody, when the old pressures come sweeping back they just go back to where they were. The moment is lost. On that day, the religious man was not there where he was needed, he was up the other end of the temple, full of his own good deeds.

What has not dawned on a lot of people, even after 2,000 years, is that pride is a worse sin than the obvious sins that make the headlines. The tax-gatherer and the prodigal son, who have obvious sins, may be closer to God than the elder brother and the pharisee who are 'decent, respectable men'.

Anybody who can cry: 'O God be merciful to me, sinner that I am' is very near to God, however big a mess he may be in. Yet we still find people who feel that they cannot come to church because they feel they are not good enough. You don't have to 'be good enough' to be a Christian. You give your life, mess and all, to Christ, so that He may redeem the mess, and eventually His goodness, the goodness of love, grows up within you.

Look at the hymn 'Just as I am without one plea . . .'

John 8:1–11

(If you are using the New English Bible, you will find this story, on its own, right at the end of St John's Gospel. Nobody is quite sure where this story belongs.)

This is a happening, not a parable. It is more understandable if you remember that Jewish teachers sat while they taught, and wrote in the dust, whereas our teachers stand and write on a blackboard. Jesus acts out God's attitude to sin; not condemning but seeking to find and rescue the lost soul.

It is a beautiful story, but with a grim side. It is a reminder that narrowly religious people tend to be very cruel, taking a delight in punishment. They come down like a ton of bricks on a sexual sin, while the man who is money-loving and proud gets away without a rebuke, especially if he might make a good contribution to church funds!

His enemies knew Jesus well. They knew that Jesus would never join in a stoning. Yet The Law laid this down as a punishment for certain types of adultery. If Jesus refused, he could be accused of law-breaking, and complicity. They thought they had him, yet his escape was so simple.

As this week's readings come to an end, we should have a clearer idea about the God who loves us *just as we are*. We are all a mixture. There is a lot of *bad* below the surface of the good, and a lot of *good* below the surface of the bad. God loves us all.

In the light of all this you can come to terms with the mixture of good and bad in yourself, without being morbid. And look again at those whose sin hurts you, and makes you want to 'cast a stone'.

Introduction

Make Love, Not War! This slogan has been very popular recently among idealists and it might well be our title for this week's reading, except that Jesus' 'love' was something far wider than what was in the minds of the hippies who made so much of this phrase.

This week's readings begin with the Love of Christ reaching out to the suffering masses of humanity, and ends with him facing tension among his neighbours and family. There are important lessons to be learned here for us today: many who set out with high ideals have seen it all crumble as they came face to face with the grim realities of human nature. Some have reduced Christianity itself to being no more than a lovely ideal, and they become very bitter later on, saying that they have lost faith. The higher you aim, the harder you fall.

'Make love, not war' was Jesus' policy, but carrying it out was hard then, as now. It involves a lot of hard thinking, a weeding out of sentimentality, a digging deep into the bedrock of truth. Shallow religion is easy to get and easy to lose. We cannot offer you the truth pre-digested, sugar-coated and painless. It doesn't come that way.

Matthew 9:35–38

When you have read this passage, stop.
Begin to use your imagination.
Build up the picture in your mind's eye.

Remember pictures you have seen on TV of struggling masses, refugees, homeless, famine areas, and so on. 'Sheep without a shepherd', what a description! At the mercy of their own stupidity, attacked by all sorts of 'wolves', aimless, bleating pitifully; that is how Jesus saw them, and still sees them. Try to see them that way too, 'with compassion' (that means literally 'suffering-with').

It is painful to see them that way, so we prefer not to look. Looking with compassion leads to feeling that we ought to *do* something about it, so we prefer to look away. But, in your mind's eye, see the Face of Jesus looking at that crowd, looking at those awkward neighbours, watching the crowds streaming into the bingo. Instead of feeling: 'It's hopeless', he sees this great harvest of human need as *opportunity*. He is beginning to think of the need for more helpers, new labourers.

Now take a walk. A walk with Jesus, looking through His eyes at the people you pass in the street. Look with *compassion*. When you get back from your walk, pray for more helpers in your own area, for people who will reach out to this great mass of sheep without a shepherd.

Matthew 10:1–4

Yesterday we read of how Jesus told those around him to pray for more helpers, and we prayed too. Today we read of how he turned to them, and he turns to us, saying more or less: 'Right, now you are going to be the answer to your own prayers!'

He began to draw together a central fellowship, and straightway he sent them out on a mission as his representatives. We would have expected him to wait until he was sure that they all understood properly, but no. Later on, we will read about how little they understood, yet Jesus sent them out all the same. To understand why, perhaps we can learn from modern educationalists who say that the best way of learning is by trying to teach. And Alcoholics Anonymous know that when an alcoholic is beginning to be sober, he must begin to try to help other alcoholics.

In the same way, we do not learn the Faith by sitting reading books . . . even this one! . . . until we know enough to go out. We will never get anywhere that way. There will always be bits we don't understand, excuses for doing nothing. We learn by *going* out in His Name.

Jesus has added your name to that list that begins with Simon Peter, and Andrew, his brother. His Power is available for us to work with, and he can work through you. Human need is so urgent that each of us must throw himself or herself into the work *now*. You will learn as you *do*. He called the church into being, as we read in these verses, because human need was so great. The need is still great, and here you are!

Luke 4:16–30

In the Jewish synagogue any adult male was expected to be able to provide comment on the Bible-reading, so naturally when Jesus returned home famous, they asked him for a sermon.

It is worth looking up the passage he read. It is in the Old Testament, the book of Isaiah chapter 61, written at least 500 years before Jesus. People used to have interesting discussions about who it referred to, and the people in the synagogue were expecting another that day. But Jesus just cut through it all: 'Today this has come true!' Just like that! What a nerve!

Note what followed: stories about how Jewish prophets had helped and healed *foreigners*. The congregation might have expected a rousing sermon on how God's Spirit had roused heroes to win battles and to slay foreigners, making the Jews the master-race. But from Jesus they get no call to arms, only a call to heal and to serve. Patriotic feeling is offended: 'Who does he think he is?'

Patriotism has its place, but also its dangers, as we see in Bob Dylan's songs about how everybody used to fight each other sure that they had 'God on their side'. It is a caricature in song of an attitude which has brought the church into much disrepute.

Jesus saw that his nation had a calling and a glory, but not in conquest. Rather it was to bring the world a knowledge of the One God of all, by being the servant of all, from being underdog, not top-dog.

What are you proud of in your nation's history?

What sort of action would you expect a Spirit-filled man to take?

Mark 3:31–35

The background to this story is that hostility towards Jesus is building up, as we have already seen. The authorities are sending officials from the capital to deal with him. Some say he is mad, some say he is bad, but hostility is rising.

Our reading takes up at verse 31 with a very human touch. His family are getting really worried. They want him to return home to his safe job as a joiner. They mean it for the best. It must have been agony for Jesus to say 'No', knowing how it would hurt his mother. Well-meaning families often get themselves hurt in this way, for the more possessive a family is, the more it puts the young person in the position where he must break right away if he is to be himself. Jesus knew this tension, and many a teenager today has been grateful that he did. It meant a break with his family, but it also meant that from that point on, blood-relationships meant nothing. His family from then on would be those who shared the work.

Even for Mary herself, what mattered was not so much that she was his mother, but rather that when God's call came she said 'Here am I; I am the Lord's servant.' It seems that later on James, his brother, and the others came round, but at the end of this reading we leave Jesus with another dark cloud in the sky, having broken with his family, but for ourselves, a vision of a new family made up of all who respond to the Love of God, as Paul said in his letter to the Galatians 3:29. Anybody who says 'Our Father' with me is my brother or sister.

Introduction

We saw in an earlier set of readings that Jesus' message could be boiled down to: 'The Kingdom of God is upon you.' We saw too, that the Jews had been expecting God's king (messiah or christ) to pop out of the sky and set up God's Kingdom on earth, solving all their problems, so that everything in the garden would once again be lovely. Some people still think like that today.

This week, then, we look at how Jesus tried to alter people's ideas about what 'The Kingdom of God' means. We look at four parables aimed at getting people to re-think ideas handed to them by the official religion of their day.

Today we often hear people say: 'Why doesn't God make people do right?' 'Why doesn't God stop wars?' We have all asked these questions, and they spring from thinking that God is like a great dictator. Jesus' teaching was that He is not like that at all. It is strange that after 2,000 years we still cling to ideas which he tried to dislodge. In fact it is worth asking yourself if your difficulty in making sense of the world, comes from trying to reconcile what you see day by day, with the picture of God which Jesus tried to dislodge. Jesus' actual teaching about God makes sense, in a way that 'the great dictator' idea of God does not.

Mark 4: 1–20

The fields of Israel were, and often still are, patches of ground on mountain sides, surrounded by thorn and cactus hedges, often with a right-of-way running through them. Therefore broadcasting seed was a dodgy business, a lot was wasted. (By the way, that is where our word 'broadcasting' originated!)

So we read this parable and ask: 'What does that tell me about the Kingdom of God?' What has it told you about how God rules the world? Jesus' phrase in verse 11 is 'The secret of God's Kingdom', or, as we would put it: The clue to how God rules the world. What is it? When He wants something done, He scatters the seed-idea all over the world, until somebody picks it up and it bears fruit.

Or change the picture to the sort of broadcasting we are more used to: God broadcasts what is needed to stop a war, but not many people are tuning in to His Broadcast. In this way man's freedom is safeguarded. He has a choice of programmes, and he can allow his mind to be filled with seed ideas of every type, as they pour in from other people, from TV, newspapers and so on. Even if he does occasionally manage to tune in to God, the seed is soon dislodged by the next TV programme.

It is when we *do* really tune in to God that His Kingdom, His Control, operates in our lives and His Will is done: 'Thy Kingdom come, Thy Will be done on earth. . . .' 'I want to be tuned in to Your Word, so that what You want will be done in my bit of the world.' Can you really say that prayer?

D

Mark 4:26–29

Look at a field of corn. Each day it looks much the same as it did the previous day. It takes a real expert to see the difference each day. In the same way, a casual observer cannot see that God is doing anything in the world, and there certainly seems to be little sign of the sort of Kingdom the Jews were expecting.

In this parable, then, Jesus points to slow growth as a secret of the Kingdom, so slow as to be almost negligible. But, just because it is slow, it does not mean that we need give up and think that nothing is happening.

This parable says that one day *harvest-time* will come. God will say: 'Enough.' It is foolish to try to guess how and when, as the sects often do. But, as Burns said: 'It's coming yet for a' that.'

The papers with the highest circulation nearly always stress the sensational, the wicked, the disastrous. The slow development of Christian love and service is not news. Churches, and bodies like the United Nations, only hit the news when something goes wrong. To find the good they are doing is not easy...you have to find magazines and circulars which are not easy to get.

There are signs of hope in the world, for those with eyes to see them, and you are becoming part of that process of slow growth. Take courage, and know that one day 'The Harvest', whatever that may mean, will come. 'Know that your work is not in vain, in the Lord', as St Paul said.

Mark 4: 30–34

Another blow at the idea that when God acts, it must be something sensational. Isaiah, writing 500 years earlier cried out: 'Oh! If only you would tear the heavens and come down, so that the mountains would flow at your coming!' We can sympathize with his impatience with God's slow way of working. He wanted something big, and he wanted it *now*.

But, remember the story of Jesus' Temptations that we read in Week 2? He rejected the spectacular way. God starts working from something tiny, like the mustard-seed, the Jewish illustration of smallness: 'As small as a mustard seed'. *Small beginnings* is the rule: a baby in a manger in a remote Judean village, the chance meeting of neighbours, these are God's way of starting something big.

In our own lives too, it is very often something quite small and down to earth that begins our new direction in life. Spectacular conversions are the exception, not the rule. That is why the Christian never writes off any incident in his life as trivial. Time and again we find that a grain of mustard seed was slipped in among very humdrum events, and from that small beginning, rooted in everyday events, a vast spreading network of results flows. In our parable the birds, representing that which lies far beyond the little garden, come to roost in the grown mustard plant.

It is easy to look for God in the wrong places, and then wonder why we never find Him. Jesus teaches us to look in the insignificant places, at small things you might easily miss. Learn this, and life can never be dull!

Luke 6:46–49

It is only too easy to sing hymns, say creeds, go to church and build up a decent life, but on the wrong foundations. That leads to tragedy. Too many people have never really worked out their faith. They have accepted what some-body taught them as children, without really *digging deep* as adults. Then, in one of the storms of life, their whole 'house' collapses around them, and they complain that they have lost faith. The more splendid the house of life that you build, the more tragic it is when it collapses.

But now, as you read this, you are 'digging deep'. And this process of looking after the foundations must go on throughout life. Jesus never said that if we followed him, we would escape the storms of life. Perhaps we wish that he would say that! Some people *do* go to church in the hope that it will bring them better luck! He *does* say that if we dig deep and really base our lives on His Word, we will be able to stand up in those storms of life when everything moveable gets blown away.

Now, how about taking a walk, or spending an evening by the fire, going over all you have read so far. Are you papering over the cracks with religious paper, or are you renewing the foundations?

Introduction

This week we look at four miracles. Modern people find miracles a problem, yet they are an inseparable part of the Gospel story. Each of them is told vividly, with little details—such as only an eye-witness would put in. It is possible that if you or I had been there, we might have retold the story rather differently, yet many of us believe that these were real happenings.

Many of us who have been involved in the healing ministry have experienced the Lord's power to heal, and we take these stories of healing seriously. Our experiences are perhaps on a lower scale, but we know that these stories do not need to be explained away, as some people would wish.

But what is a miracle? The men who wrote the Gospels used three words: *a work; a sign; a power*. These words are rather different from the English word 'miracle', and they did not suggest that Jesus broke the laws of nature. The words *work* and *power* indicate that real effort was involved. When man discovers a new sort of power, and makes it work, he does things that would once have been thought impossible, a miracle. So Jesus' *works* (let's get away from the word 'miracle') were a *sign* that something new was coming into the world, that a new *power* was being released.

The Love we see in Jesus is creative power, and when it flows through a human life, mankind is able to rise to new heights. So Jesus' work was natural for a Son of God, and it should come naturally to all children of God. His works were a sign of hope for us all, that there are heights of life we little dream of, possibilities greater than we imagine, if we learn to forget ourselves, follow Him, concerned above all to express His Love in the world.

Mark 5:1–20

What a strange•story! It gets even stranger when you look at it carefully. Nobody made this up for propaganda purposes! It began with an attempt to get away for some peace, crossing the lake into foreign territory. But there was no escape, the madman saw to that! Since it had been evening when they started their journey, it might have been 9 or 10 o'clock when they met him, and the story ends in daylight, so it had taken all night.

In verse 8 there is a strange detail: 'Jesus was saying' . . . (the imperfect tense, for the grammatically minded!), suggesting that in this case it was not just 'one word from Jesus and that was that'. A real, prolonged struggle was going on through those midnight hours. Another strange detail is that Jesus tried to find the name of the demon, the only case in which he did so, although it was the usual practice as we saw in the story in Week 3 Day 4.

A modern psychiatrist suggested that perhaps the man's village had been massacred by a Roman legion and he had survived, but the memory still went round and round in his head, the tramp of the legion, the fear, the hatred, the thousand emotions that such experiences leave behind. Hence he says that his demon is *legion*. That is one idea.

The incident with the pigs is puzzling too. But animals are very sensitive to psychic things, and as they came sniffing around in the dawn, it is not unlikely that they would have taken fright and charged off, over the cliff. Perhaps Jesus said: 'There is your legion, running away from you. It will never trouble you again.' (It is worth noting that in modern experience, animals have reacted strangely when psychic phenomena have happened.)

However we understand this flesh-creeping story, it speaks to us of a Jesus who takes infinite trouble with people, even when he is tired himself. This healing was *work* . . . hard work. All the thanks he got was to be asked to leave.

Mark 5:21–43

This story follows on from the one we read yesterday. Back on his own side of the lake there is another emergency. But this story is a happy one, bathed in sunlight.

At the heart of the story are the words he spoke to the sleeping, or as we would say 'comatose', girl: *talitha cumi*. These words are in the dialect that was spoken in Galilee, and are what any mother might say to her daughter any morning. 'Up you get lassie' might render it best. It was so natural and simple, no long prayers, no ritual, just a homely act. No wonder it stuck in their memories so vividly that it comes to us in the actual dialect words he used. Then, he brought them down to earth by telling them to get something to eat.

Then, right in the middle of the story comes this other one about the woman suffering from haemorrhages. According to Jewish law she was unclean and would defile anybody she touched, so she had defiled Jesus by touching him. No wonder she was scared when he asked who it was. Notice that Jesus was not satisfied that she should be healed, she had to know *Him*. It might have been faith healing or superstition if he had let it go at that. Spiritual healing goes on to give a personal relationship with God.

In this story too, we see that he was aware that power had gone out of him, and this reminds us that healing is *work*. It includes giving *yourself*. Like any craftsman, he made it look easy, but there is more to it than meets the eye. In the church today we are rediscovering the meaning of healing, but it is not something to be dabbled with. We have to learn his simplicity (that's difficult!), his self-giving, his involvement with the crowds of suffering people.

One might say that the Christian life *is* healing, with each Christian having a part to play, not just the doctors and nurses, but the whole body of Christian people concerned with the healing of mankind. Within that work, you will have some special part to play. That is your life.

Mark 7:24–30

Here is another story that is rather puzzling, obviously not just made up for propaganda purposes. This story, too, begins with Jesus trying to get away from it all. He is in 'foreign territory' where he can expect freedom from the crowds, time to have some peace with his 'apprentices'. Yet even here he cannot escape, as this woman comes up with her request. Can you understand Jesus' hesitation? One healing leads to another, and another, and so on. Perhaps there was a real temptation to turn his back on the Jews and look further afield. Perhaps the vision of a world healing mission?

So we have his surprising reply, seemingly so uncharacteristic. Yet one point makes it a little more understandable; we have discovered that the Phoenicians were the only people in that part of the world who kept dogs as pets, instead of regarding them as scavengers. The word Jesus used is not the word 'dog' but 'doggie', an affectionate diminutive.

However, whatever the wider issues at stake, and whatever the reason behind Jesus' reply, the woman's sense of humour and her insistence won through. Her daughter is already healed. By the way, we have many cases in our own experience when somebody got better at the very moment people were praying for them. We call it 'absent healing'.

Notice how varied Jesus' approach was; in this case he did not need to go to the house; whereas in the case of Jairus' daughter he did. You can follow that up, seeing how each case was dealt with individually; there were no magic formulae, no set rituals. Anybody who follows the Lord in the work of healing, must learn to become sensitive to the needs of the person, and sensitive to God's Will, so that the right thing may be done in each case. 'May Your Kingdom come into this situation, so that Your Will may be done for this suffering soul.'

Mark 8:1–10

Many who accept that Jesus healed the sick, still find this, and other nature miracles, hard to stomach. Yet all four Gospels report this story, in fact St Mark has another story like it in chapter 6.

Some have tried to understand it by suggesting that Jesus began sharing the little they had, with the result that all who had been hiding their packed lunches for fear of having to share got them out, and there was enough to go round with some to spare. They suggest the miracle was in terms of overcoming human fear and greed, rather than over matter. Others accept that the Lord *did* do for others, what he had refused to do for himself in the desert (Week 2 Day 4).

It is when John tells the story (John 6:1–15) that we get another hint, one that has taken on new meaning in the light of what we have learned from the Dead Sea Scrolls and other literature of the time. In verse 15 John tells that the crowd saw this as a clear claim to be the King, the Messiah, and Jesus found himself with an explosive political situation on his hands. Jesus turned away from being the sort of king the nationalists wanted, and that would have made them bitter and hostile. It was a turning point for him.

Sharing bread is always an explosive issue. We tend to want to have next week's cake assured, before we really get down to thinking of sharing bread with the hungry multitudes. Our concern is not really: *Give us this day our daily bread*. But if our world does not learn to share bread soon, we are going to face world starvation and bloodshed. As somebody said: 'There is enough to meet man's need, but not enough to satisfy man's greed.'

And another point: Can we be realistic in praying for the sick when a lot of disease comes from eating too much of the wrong sort of food, while others starve? 'Give us all our daily bread; never mind my cake just now, Lord.'

Introduction

Mark Twain once commented that what bothered him about the Bible, was not the things he did not understand, but the things he *did*.

This week we look at the things which Jesus said to his 'apprentices' as he tried to train them to take their places in the Kingdom of God. They are shattering. Perhaps it would be easier to keep them beautifully wrapped up in old English, because that way they don't seem to be part of our world. But let us look at them in their challenging modern form, and if we take them seriously perhaps it will lead to a genuine Jesus Revolution.

Luke 6:20–26

But that's ridiculous, Lord!
It upsets all our ideas about who's happy
        and who isn't.
There are too many hungry, poor, weeping people
        in the world,
and we don't want to be like them;
in fact we're glad we are not.
We want a higher standard of living;
we want to be laughing.
The commercials tell us how to be happy,
they tell us how much we need before we can be happy.

There's just one thing bothers us,
somehow we don't seem to be all that much happier
        than our forefathers were,
even though we have so much more than they had.

Everything around us tells us that Jesus is
        talking nonsense,
but what if he is right, and the commercials are wrong?
To be sitting pretty, laughing your head off,
while God is among the refugees and the oppressed
        would be sitting on dynamite, if Jesus is right.
To be over-feeding my body,
polluting the world with leftovers
        while God is among the starving,
would be asking for trouble if Jesus is right.

To be among the 'successes' in a world in which
        God is among the 'failures'
is a ghastly error, if Jesus is right.

Perhaps this is the sort of place where you stop reading
the Bible. Or perhaps it is time to have a long think about
a lot of things we take for granted.

Luke 6:27–35

Yesterday was bad enough, today is worse!
For two thousand years Christians have quietly
    ignored this passage:
'No disrespect, Lord, but you know what we mean.'

There is only one snag,
    violence is begetting violence,
    weapons become so terrible that they
        cannot be used any more;
    the end of life on this planet is possible.

Is there no other way? Nobody is suggesting that it is
easy just to switch over to the Jesus-way to solve it all, but
isn't it time we began to take this seriously? We begin by
working out in small ways how to overcome evil by good,
and work up to the big world-wide problems. If we try this
on our own, we shall soon be disheartened, but Jesus said
this to men who were sharing life together, and working it
out together. In the church we should be helping each
other in the battle against evil, praying for each other's
enemies, working out how to tackle the various forms of
evil we face.

It will take as much thought and work as old-fashioned
warfare, and there will be casualties too! Yet, how often do
we find this sort of thing on the syllabus in church-groups?
In fact often such groups are notorious for their petty
feuds. Each Christian group should be a peace-research
centre, in which people are experimenting with the Jesus
way, tackling evil in His Name and with His Love,
reconciling people across the barriers men have erected.

How about it?

Luke 6:36–37 and 41–42

Now Jesus is attacking one of the favourite human games: Finding Fault. It makes you feel good when you can show that somebody who is well-respected is really no better than you. The more you feel a 'heel', the more strongly you feel the need to criticize the people who rub it into you by being popular and successful. The more you feel that you are a failure, the more it is a necessity to show that it is really others that are to blame, and that is *they* who are rotten, not you. The bigger the plank sticking out of your own eye, the greater the fuss you need to make of the speck in your brother's.

Once again, the church is not very successful in getting this over; in fact it seems to be a very critical, guilt-creating body in the eyes of most people. Church folk enjoy a good denouncing sermon, straight from the shoulder, one that makes people (other people) squirm. Sermons attacking bingo, Roman Catholics, permissiveness are popular in many quarters. Yet the man who criticizes others always reveals his own weakness, if only he knew it. The church which sat in judgment on others, has now been found wanting by most people and is ignored.

We have seen that God looks at us human-beings as wrecks that need to be salvaged, and he asks us to look on our fellow-wrecks with the same compassion as he does. 'Be compassionate as your Father is.' We are all in this together, and all we can say is: 'Lord don't lead us into temptation without delivering us from evil.' Who knows which of us will slip next? We all need to pray that prayer.

Whom do you tend to criticize most? What does that tell you about yourself? Spend some time making a list of the people you are critical of, and try to see them as God sees them.

Luke 6:43–45

Real goodness comes from the inside, not from the outside, that is what Jesus seems to be saying here. You may frighten people away from doing some kinds of wrong, sometimes. But you can't frighten them into goodness. You can't even change yourself, any more than a thistle could produce a nice juicy fig, however much it wanted to! Even if we have really taken in this week's readings, and are really determined to turn over a new leaf, we would still fail. Something more than good intentions is needed.

We have to experience a change right deep down in our inner beings, 'in our hearts' as the Bible puts it.

That change is the result of *love*. When people begin to love, they begin to behave differently. The deeper the love the more radical the change. Christianity is not telling you to change, to love your enemies, to want to be poor, and so on. . . . The Gospel says: This is what God is like, love *Him* and you will begin to grow into people who will naturally produce the fruits of the Christian life.

So many people have tried idealistically to live the Christian life and have failed miserably, ending up disillusioned. They have neglected the basic command 'Love God'. A great Christian once prayed: 'Lord Jesus, merciful Redeemer, Friend and Brother, may we see you more clearly, love you more dearly and follow you more nearly.'

See him, love him, follow him: that is the order. Make that prayer your own.

Introduction

This week's readings take us away to the north of
Palestine, into foreign territory as far as the disciples were
concerned. It was in the area that leads up to Mount
Hermon, the massive snow-covered hill.

Why was Jesus abroad? Did the events we read about in
Week 9 Day 4 make him feel the need to get the disciples
away by themselves to try to get them to understand?
Whatever the reason, it meant that the events we read
about this week begin the long walk to Jerusalem which
will end on the Cross. From now on Jesus speaks a lot
about his coming death.

So often we have scattered bits and pieces of Jesus' life
lying around in our lives, like a jigsaw we have never tried
to make up. Perhaps it would be a good thing to look back
over our readings so far to see if the actual story is fitting
together and making up a picture.

Have you followed Jesus' struggle to get people to
understand what He means by 'The Kingdom'? Have you
followed the mounting opposition: priests, politicians, ordinary people, and so on? Have you noticed Jesus's
problem with supporters who wanted the wrong thing?

The events we read about this week show that the time
had come 'to sort out the men from the boys', and perhaps
the events we read about in the papers and see on TV
mean that our day is such a time too. A hazy goodwill
towards a 'gentle Jesus meek and mild' won't stand the test
of our day. In the face of a world which becomes more
violent each day, we have to decide whose side we are on.
Perhaps this week's readings will clarify this.

Mark 8:27–33

Jesus confronts his friends with the key question, the question which still haunts men and women 2,000 years later:

Who on earth is this man Jesus?

He introduces the topic gently, asking what other people were saying about him. Some, it seems, thought that he was a reincarnation of some great Biblical figure, some thought of him as a great preacher, and so on. It made an interesting discussion, then as now.

Then he faced them with *the* issue: 'Who do you say that I am?' Earlier on they could have given the answer glibly (see Week 3 Day 1), but now it was not so easy. Jesus had thrown away a golden opportunity to claim the kingship (Week 9 Day 4), he was losing public support as well as incurring the anger of the religious authorities. He did not seem to be doing anything, apart from healing and teaching, and that was not what the messiah was expected to do. No, it was no longer easy to say you still believed that he was the long-awaited king.

Then Simon Peter blurted it out, only to be told to keep quiet about it. Jesus then went on to explain that while he was indeed the messiah, he was not going to lead armies and kill Romans, in fact the Romans would kill him.

Peter was shocked. This did not make sense, so he began to rebuke Jesus, but in doing so he was voicing one of Jesus' temptations, and he got a real shock. He had meant well, after all!

For us too, in the midst of continuous debate, we need to make our stand: Who do you say Jesus is? The discussions will go on till doomsday. It's no use waiting for an answer from 'the experts'. Even if, like Peter, you are a bit confused, yet still either you believe he is *the answer*, and you stake your bottom dollar, your shirt and all on that, or you stay on the side-lines.

Mark 8:34–38

This is a shattering passage, and it must have been even more shattering for those first few loyal followers. It was another blow to their great hope that Jesus was going to be the messiah they were hoping for. It is a passage which startles anybody who stops to think, and the New English Bible version of it is very worth studying. A cross in those days just meant a gallows, a public gallows, and it was considered the most degrading form, as well as the most agonising form, of execution. A really modern version of these famous words would be: 'If you are going to follow me, you might as well tie the noose round your neck now!'

(How easily people wear the cross as a decoration! In one secondary school there was a craze among the youngsters to wear a gallows on their blazer lapels. People were horrified, yet a cross is far more horrible than a modern gallows.)

Then there is that phrase 'Deny yourself' or 'Leave self behind'. It is just the opposite of 'assert yourself', 'do your own thing' and such advice. Unfortunately many of us have come across forms of 'self-denial' that were only an upside-down way of self-assertion, so we tend to write off what Jesus says here.

Of course, Jesus could have put things more reasonably and simply, but he deliberately said these shocking things to jog us into re-thinking. Because you probably disagree with them at first, you will find yourself remembering them. But stop and think: Can you think of examples of people who have played safe, taken the line of least resistance, and lived to be a wash-out?

Think of times when life has really been worth living; has it not always been when you had 'lost yourself' in something outside yourself, something greater than yourself? In the long run, my whole personality, built up over the years to help me to 'get on in the world', must be broken up, and then the true self can emerge at last.

E

Mark 9:2–10

To understand this passage, we must look ahead a bit. From that mountain-top onwards, Jesus' face would be set towards Jerusalem and death. Peter's confession of faith, mixed up though it had been, had been a critical point, and now Jesus knew that the time had come to face the climax of his mission.

Do you wonder that the Lord headed for the high hills? Do you wonder, either, that he gathered around him those who were closest to him? If you look back to the story of his baptism, which we read in Week 2, you will see that the two experiences have a lot in common, only this time it was Peter, James and John who heard The Voice.

What about the radiance? Well, perhaps it is puzzling. Was it that the three of them *saw* the truth shining out on this occasion, whereas usually they saw only another man? Or was there a radiance on this occasion that was not normally there? We are not told which it was. Yet it has been known for a radiance to be seen around some great souls while they were praying. The fact that Moses, representing The Law, and Elijah, representing The Prophets, were seen with him discussing his 'exodus'—that is the word used—is fascinating.

Peter's reaction is so out of place that it is almost comic. His immediate reaction, as a practical man, is to *do* something: build three shelters. A silly thing to say? But remember Peter was telling the story against himself!

So we have read the disciples' confession of faith and their vision of the Lord's glory. Probably we would have expected the events to have happened the other way round: the vision first, then the confession of faith. People want the vision first, before they step out in faith, whereas we get moments of insight and vision *after* we have taken the step of faith.

Verses 9 and 10 remind us that for the disciples, this vision made it seem even more inconceivable that Jesus should be killed.

Mark 9:14–29

What a come-down! After that mountain-top experience, they are right back to earth, with the disciples failing to do the Lord's work, and the crowd seething around. That is the way in life: a mountain-top experience is followed by a bumpy arrival down to earth.

Once again we notice Jesus' way of working. This time he starts asking questions about the background, and the father gets impatient. Then Jesus begins to work on the father, and in desperation the man gives vent to one of the greatest prayers: 'Lord I believe, help thou mine unbelief', 'I have faith, help me where faith falls short'. That prayer was enough for Jesus. We do not need to hide from him the strange mixture of faith and doubt inside us. Real faith puts the whole mixed-up mess of emotions into his hands, and leaves it there. Perhaps you could not say you believed every point of Christian doctrine, but you could echo the father's cry?

Notice that the boy has an extra bad fit, and then passes out. This has been noticed in modern cases too: an immediate worsening of the condition before complete healing.

'Why did we fail?' ask the disciples. We too sometimes wonder why people don't get better when we pray for them. Often we pass the buck on to God, saying: 'It was not His Will to heal.' Then we accept that the illness is His Will. But not Jesus. If the boy was still ill, it was because a deeper level of prayer was needed in a difficult case like this. Some cases were more difficult than others, calling for a 'higher voltage' of the Power of God. It is the same today.

Many people who have accepted their illness as God's Will may actually be ill because the disciples today are so barren in prayer. One factor could be the church's prayer-failure. How much time does your church or group spend in prayer?

Introduction

The experts often discuss how early in his life Jesus knew that he was to be executed, an apparent failure. Some think he knew it all along, others think that at first he expected success, then expected eventual success, and only realized later that he was to be 'despised and rejected by men'.

That is the sort of discussion that goes on in theological circles. ('Theology' is the systematic thinking about God.) We wait in vain for any final answer that theologians would all agree to. But most of them would agree that by the time Jesus set his face to Jerusalem, he knew the fate which awaited him, and he went, not as a victim caught up on the wheels of fate, but deliberately.

Let us remember that Jesus was fully human. Over these past weeks we have seen that clearly: he was a real man. He felt the need for fellowship, and gathered his friends round him at times of crisis. He was tempted to court popularity. He knew the attraction of home, safety and a steady job. He wanted to *live*. As we follow his journey southwards, we shall see his loneliness increasing, his friends quarrelling more and understanding him less. He knew that he was going to lead them into terrible disappointment and desolation. He knew his popularity was waning, and the net was closing in.

We may say 'But he knew it was foretold in the Bible.' You know that going to the dentist will not really hurt much, and you know you will be better off with that cavity filled, but ...! So now we follow his walk south, a walk taking some months, and watch his inner and outer struggle which culminated on the cross.

Mark 9:30–32

In these few verses we get quite a thumb-nail sketch of what was going on. It tells us that he has come down from the mountains to the hills of Galilee, and it tells us the sort of teaching he was giving the twelve. He was trying to get them to look afresh at the Bible as they knew it, written by the prophets centuries earlier. There were—and still are, of course!—plenty of verses in which the promise seems to be that God's Kingdom will be an empire with the Jews as the master-race. Look, for instance, at the central verses of Isaiah 61. The Jews were steeped in these promises, their whole faith centred on God's Kingdom coming like this. But Jesus kept on referring to other passages, like Isaiah 53. If you look this up you will find that it is hard to realize that it was written many centuries before Jesus.

Sometimes people today says that Jesus' teaching was basically simple. The disciples did not find it simple. They could not take it in, as it cut right across all that they had grown up to believe. By the time, months later, Jesus went to the cross, they still had not taken it in. So we see Jesus walking along, trying to find understanding from his friends, trying to prepare them for the ordeal ahead. But they just became confused and frightened.

Do they seem very stupid? Are we sure that we do not cling, more than we realize, to man-made theories of 'religion', so that we do not hear what Jesus is really saying? Do we take in what Jesus says to us today about taking 'the way of the cross'?

Are you just puzzled? Like them?

Mark 9:33–37

Their journey has brought them to their home-town of Capernaum, and although they do not realize it, it is Jesus' farewell visit.

There is an old tradition that the child referred to in verse 36 was Peter's. Notice that Mark tells us that 'Jesus put his arms round him' . . . just a little detail the other two Gospel writers leave out. But remember that Mark's Gospel is Peter's secretary writing down what Peter used to say, and it all comes to life! How vividly Peter would remember the Lord's last visit in the flesh to his home, and how vividly he would remember Jesus standing there with his arms round the lad.

However we get another vivid picture that is less pleasant! Feeling that the great moment lies ahead, they are jockeying for position, and yet they know it is wrong to do so, and are silent when Jesus challenges them about their discussion.

What a lovely object lesson Jesus gave them! His Kingdom, in which they were hoping for top places, was an upside-down kingdom, in which the servant is the king, and the child more important than church dignitaries and civil powers.

They missed the point. So do we. But Jesus made something of them eventually, so there is hope for us!

Mark 10:1–12

The scene is set in what we call Jordan, which shows that Jesus was taking the long route to Jerusalem, and we have the religious leaders trying to get Jesus involved in one of their interminable arguments about the various rules and regulations that made up religion as they knew it. What were reasonable grounds for divorce? One school of thought said that if a woman spoiled her man's dinner, that was grounds for him to give her a note and send her packing. Others thought that adultery was the only ground. What did Jesus think?

To understand this, you have to realize that 'divorce' meant something quite different in those days. To begin with there was no way a woman could divorce a man on any ground at all, so it is strange that Jesus should speak as if there were. Then a divorced woman had no way of earning a living, except on the streets. A man had only to give the woman a note saying he divorced her, and she was deprived of home, family, decency, and probably would starve, with no hope of redress. Divorce for them meant a man's right to discard his wife. We are thinking of something quite different when we ask what protection a woman has against a violent boor of a husband.

Jesus' answer goes back to fundamentals. The husband–wife relationship is part of the stuff of creation, meant to be even closer than the parent–child relationship. For the Jews it was the father–son relationship which really mattered, and the woman was a mere means to that end. Jesus altered this, and the church ever since has stuck to the husband–wife relationship as being the prime one. Jesus was revolutionary here.

In our day it seems as though now that the Man–God relationship is missing, the man–woman relationship is also going, and marriages seem to break up so often that the happy one is the exception rather than the rule. Once marriage becomes a mere legal convenience, not something sacramental, the foundations of life are threatened.

Mark 10:13–16

This is a favourite story, especially in Sunday School. It is so well known that we miss the 'bite' in it. From the point of view of his disciples, Jesus was having an important theological discussion with important people. They hoped that Jesus would make a good impression, and the last thing they wanted was that he should be interrupted by the chatter of kids. No wonder they tried to get rid of this interruption.

Once again Jesus upset their ideas as to what is really important in *his* kingdom. It is more important to meet and bless these children than it is to discuss divorce with their elders and betters. Theological debate must give way to real encounter. Jesus also came back to one of his favourite themes: the way forward in his Kingdom is through being taken back to square one, being born again, becoming poor in spirit, and now becoming like one of these little children.

A few months later, having deserted, denied and lost their Lord, the disciples would really know what this meant. They would then know that they knew nothing, and would be stripped down to what Alcoholics Anonymous call 'rock bottom'. Then things could begin to happen.

We need not be afraid of the things which humiliate us, and take us back to square one. The man of the world dreads this more than anything, but the Christian knows that it is a prelude to a new birth, to a resurrection.

Think back over this week's readings. Work out the upside-downness of Jesus' teaching. Work out whether you think his way or the world's way.

Introduction

This week we read of four conversations which Jesus had on the road, two of them with the twelve, the other two with people who were not in the inner band.

Jesus' way of handling questions may seem strange to us, but there is a reason for it. If you ask a factual question, such as: 'What was the date of the battle of Bannockburn?' Then the answer is '1314', and you know the date. But even if you tell a person a spiritual truth they do not *know* it until they have worked it out for themselves. A lot of people who know the right theological answers, and can quote the Bible backwards, live self-centred, materialistic lives. So it is no use just giving people the right answers, you have to stimulate them into thinking it out for themselves.

A lot of people want their religion predigested, and ready packaged in attractive wrappings, but spiritual truth does not come that way. There used to be catechisms, which were a series of questions and answers covering the basic doctrines of the faith. There was a lot to be said for them, but they could mislead people into thinking that because they 'knew all the answers' they knew it all.

Each of us has to work out the faith in our own words, through our own experience. No one teacher, no one book can give us all the answers.

Mark 10:32–45

Use your imagination to build this story into an episode in a TV play on the life of Jesus. He is striding grimly down the dusty road, with the twelve some way behind, and the crowd behind them. They are puzzled and a little over-awed. Every now and then Jesus stops to allow them to catch up, and he tries to get through to them, but it is no use, so he turns and walks on again.

Then John and James catch up to make their request. A king's right- and left-hand men were what we call prime minister and chancellor of the exchequer. The brothers are staking their claim to the plum jobs when he is king. A flaming row follows, and just imagine Jesus' face. If they had *begun* to listen to his teaching, they would never have had this argument at all. The 'throne' that is awaiting in Jerusalem is a gallows, the crown is of thorns, and the men on his right hand and left will be criminals. With grim humour Jesus points out that it will not be his verdict that decides who will be on his left and right in Jerusalem.

Patiently, wearily, he tries to give another lesson on the upside-downness of his Kingdom, but it is no use. They will only listen to their own ambition, and to the national-istic ideas implanted in them from youth.

Note what Jesus says about greatness. To be great in this world usually requires luck and ruthlessness. The true greatness of his Kingdom is open to anybody, no matter how simple or socially handicapped.

What are the status symbols in your neighbourhood? At your work? What are your ways of boosting your ego? Have you found the blessed relief of seeing it the Jesus way?

Luke 10:25–37

We have here what is perhaps the best known of all Jesus' stories. Its meaning is clear, and does not need much explanation, but its setting does. The lawyer's question was a stock one, often discussed by religious experts. Our version might be:

What is the top priority in life?

Before you go into the Bible answer, check your own priorities.

Jesus did not give a pat answer, but threw it back at the man, who gave one of the stock answers, which happened to be the right one, so Jesus agrees with him. But he wants more than that. His questions boil down to 'Where do I draw the line?' You can't love *all* your neighbours like that! Should it be your next-door neighbour? Or those in the same town? We have to arrange some sort of priority in our obligation to love. Jesus' answer is to put the lawyer into the position of having to admit that on occasion, even a hated Samaritan could be neighbour to a Jew. Love's priority thinks in terms of *need*, not of proximity or of nationality.

Notice that the priest and levite would have been ritually defiled if they had touched a dead man, and therefore not allowed to take part in the temple ritual, so they took no risk of defiling themselves before God, as they understood it. Very reasonable, from their point of view! From Jesus' point of view they were more defiled by passing a sufferer by, than they would have been by touching a corpse.

'Go and do likewise' sounds easy, but remember that this sort of action would have been a breach of professional etiquette. Check over your priorities in the light of all this.

Luke 10:38–42

Jesus has now come to within a day's walk of Jerusalem, though it seems that he spent some months around here, more or less based on this home.

It is no surprise to us that Mary should sit at the Lord's feet listening. But in those days a woman was meant to know her place: in the kitchen. Religion was a serious subject, for men only! A sympathetic ear must have meant a lot to Jesus at this point. Yet Martha had her point of view too; she had to feed this crowd, and you can imagine her fuming among the pots and pans as she saw Mary sitting doing nothing.

It is a pity that no English translation gets the humour in Jesus' answer. He actually said that Mary has chosen the best *dish*, and she was not going to have it snatched away. Mary was doing more for Jesus by *listening* than if she had been clattering around the kitchen.

How often, after a death, people wish that they had *listened* more, and had spent more time just enjoying the other's company. They regret bitterly that they were too busy, and realize that their priorities were wrong. In church too, people are often so busy running round organizing things and attending committees, that they have no time to spend quietly in His presence. Then, when a crisis comes, they find that for all their churchiness they have no real relationship with Jesus.

We leave this story remembering that Jesus gave women a place in his circle that was quite new. Later the church tended to put women back in the conventional place, but at least we are beginning to catch up with the Lord's attitude . . . or are we?

And how about your *listening*? To loved ones? To the Lord?

Luke 11:1–10

We usually use the version of the Lord's Prayer in Matt. 6:9–13, but the last thing Jesus ever meant was for us to have a set prayer to gabble through.

His story indicates that prayer must have real determination behind it. It would have raised a laugh when he told it; as the poor man, bedded down in the midst of his family Palestinian style, had to get up, waking all the kids, cursing the friend he was usually glad to see.

The 'outline-prayer' which Jesus gives begins with the word 'abba' which is nearer our word 'dad' than the formal 'Father'. He is *our* Abba, and that sets prayer within the context of the whole family of God. We go on to think of how we want everybody to know and love Him, for that is what 'Hallowed be Thy Name' means. We think about what he has taught us about the Kingdom of God, and of how we can establish on earth God's rule of love, for if people did His Will on earth, then earth would be heaven! We bring before him the family's needs for daily bread, not just '*my* daily bread'. This involves down-to-earth concerns.

Lastly we think of ourselves as weak, muddled creatures, in need of forgiveness from God and from each other. We have to ask Him 'Please don't lead us into testing situations without delivering us from the evil to which we are prone.' This admission of our own weakness, and the assurance: 'we forgive others' leaves us in the right attitude to God and to other people. The church later added a final note of praise 'For thine is the Kingdom . . . etc.', for one should always end on a note of praise.

This outline of prayer is very different from the 'shopping-list' of requests, the pleading with a distant God, or from running through endless repetitions. It is God-centred prayer, instead of man-centred or self-centred prayer.

How does this compare with how you pray, or with how you used to pray?

Introduction

We break from the story for a week, just to sit at Jesus' feet, and listen to the sort of things he used to say.

If you are a church person, you will find it all very familiar, and perhaps you enjoy hearing it read in the beautiful language of the Authorized Version. But the very associations we have with this passage, may hide from us the terrific things that Jesus was saying. Let us take them carefully and really digest them this time.

If you are a newcomer to the Faith, you will be shattered at how the appearance of the ordinary congregation seems to be quite inconsistent with Jesus' revolutionary teaching, rather like people carrying dynamite in pretty little flowery bags.

This week Jesus points us to a new life-style, and if ever the world needed people with a new life-style, it is today. The world is waiting for Christians to work out what Jesus says here, and in the meantime things are going from bad to worse. In fact many people have given up waiting for the Church and have tried to work it out humanistically.

This is time to wake up!

Luke 12:13–21

A man appeals to Jesus to settle a family quarrel about a will. It is the sort of situation which still happens. Jesus refuses to be drawn in. His answer is a story, again.

This story is about the sort of man both brothers would have wanted to be: a material success. It attacks the outlook which led to the quarrel. Jesus goes for the root of the trouble: basic attitudes.

Can you make up a modern version? Big business man ...mergers ... new premises ... coronary thrombosis ... and that's it. What does it tell you?

Note that the Bible never suggests that God wants us to be poor and miserable. Over and over again it asserts that God wants His Family to enjoy the good things He has made so long as: (1) we do not forget Him, (2) we do not forget the needs of others. (Look up Deuteronomy 8:5–18 in which we are warned about the dangers of a rising standard of living.)

We who live in the wealthy part of the world need to think hard about this parable. It is no longer only ministers who warn us against the dangers of high living, it is doctors, scientists, economists etc. The danger to the environment and the future of the whole race are topics which must be discussed at every level. We have to ask whether our higher standard of living has brought us closer to God and made us *better* men than our fathers.

But to come back to the story we began with: it is the things we quarrel about which show us what we really think important. Where lay the roots of your last family quarrel? The last quarrel in your church?

Luke 12:22–31

As you read this, remember that Jesus, and the people he was speaking to, lived in a society in which there was no social security, no health service. They knew plenty of people who had been reduced to selling their families or even themselves into slavery, or else becoming beggars.

Therefore, to say this sort of thing was even more daring than it would be to say it today, to people who live in a welfare state. Verse 31 gives us the clue, though. Jesus is not suggesting that we sit back in a rosy, religious dream, waiting for God to drop food into our mouths. He says that if we throw ourselves into the work for the Kingdom of God, then Our Father will see to it that we have what we need to keep us going. The message is that we can get on with the work to which Jesus calls us *without worry.*

Of course there *are* times when the Christian has to take his place among the refugees and the victims of oppression; and remember that eventually Jesus himself died in agony, tortured by the heat of the sun, forced to cry out 'I thirst' and knowing only the relief of death.

But the main message of the passage is clear: God knows our material needs, and can be trusted to make sure that we have what we really need, so long as we are in tune with his purposes. Our Father means us to enjoy our food and drink and clothes, and these are His invention anyway! We are not to think that He is not interested in such things. But we are not to waste our precious lives:

> Eating in order to work,
> Working in order to eat, and so on and on.

Our Father put us here for a purpose, and we can give ourselves to that without worry. Many of us can testify as to how wonderfully God provides.

Luke 12:32–34

One or two thumbnail sketches from modern experience to hold in your mind as you read this passage:

The old lady had died, and all her little treasures were there gathering dust, waiting for the man with a van to come and dump them. The millionaire surveyed his Highland estate, but it gave him no joy, because his wife had left him. The man who spent his life building up his little shop, putting his whole heart into it, was broken when they opened up the supermarket, and he died soon afterwards.

Think of examples yourself.

If we set our hearts on things which, by their very nature, are 'here today and gone tomorrow', we are inviting heartbreak. Even if it seems a good thing to set your heart on, it can still mean disaster, as in the many cases of women who have 'lived for their families', only to find that when the family moves away as adults, they are left with nothing but an empty heart.

The point is that none of these things is wrong in itself, but anything which becomes top priority in life, in God's place, becomes an idol, and therefore a menace.

Two Jews who escaped from Hitler with nothing, not even clothes, said to Maud Royden, an English minister: 'We owe a lot to Hitler. He taught us that when you have nothing except God, you have more than enough.' In the long run it is the person with a relationship with God that is rich and loving, who has security and peace. All the other securities which look more practical and down to earth, are misleading in the long run.

What have you set your heart on?

F

Luke 12:35–46

Most of us like to settle down into a comfortable routine; in fact many people want their religion to be a sort of insurance policy against change. We have to admit that in spite of the Lord's teaching, the church herself tends to settle down in massive institutions, making herself secure and comfortable, forgetting the job which Jesus gave her to do.

The idea of being constantly on the alert, waiting in case God may break into the situation any moment, is quite disturbing. There is an Indian saying: 'The world is a bridge, pass over it, but do not build your house on it.' It is the same idea, that true life is being on the move, never settling, ready for action, looking for what God is up to next.

But let's face it, this sort of thing we have been reading this week is not popular religion!

Day 1 gave us the shivers, it's too grim.

Day 2 seems the opposite, too airy-fairy.

Day 3 goes against the grain of all that is dinned into us.

Day 4 is just plain unsettling.

One way or the other, we would rather forget this chapter. Yet sooner or later reality, or 'God' if you want to be honest, breaks in on us all, and then we complain that our faith is shaken, and that there is no justice in life. Perhaps this chapter should be taken seriously . . . no, not 'seriously', but perhaps 'triumphantly'?

Doctors tell us that *worry* is the main killer. The church crumbles because it forgets to do Jesus' work. Experts warn us about the pollution of the world, yet we still write this chapter off as nonsense.

It is time we woke up, isn't it?

Introduction

People often assume that religion is a private affair, purely personal, and with no great urgency. Rather like taking sugar in tea: some do, some don't.

But in the passages we read this week we see Jesus pushing the nation to the point of decision, warning the nation that its very existence was at stake. His march on Jerusalem was of crucial political concern, as well as being a religious matter. As a matter of history, about thirty years later the Jews made the very mistake which Jesus had warned them against; they had an armed rebellion against Rome, and were brutally crushed.

Reading these passages this week should be accompanied by a careful reading of a responsible newspaper, for there are times of decision for all nations, and Christ's words are a challenge to each nation in its turn.

Luke 13:1–5

The events which lie behind this reading concern the political life of the Jews at this time. The Galilaeans in the north had rebelled, and the Roman Governor had decided to teach them a lesson. The next time they arrived in the capital for a national religious festival Roman troops mingled with them in the temple court, and at a signal threw off their cloaks and massacred the pilgrims. It was the sort of situation Jesus had warned them to avoid. We read of how he received the news, and of how people asked: '*Why?*'

In his reply Jesus referred to another tragedy: we know from the history books that the Governor had a pet scheme concerned with building a great aqueduct to bring water into the city. A good idea, but anything which involved the Romans was hated, and the fact that taxes and conscripted labour were involved made it more unpopular. Some of it had collapsed on the workers, killing them.

So here was a problem: some people were killed because they rose against Rome, some were killed collaborating with Rome. This did not make sense to Jews who had the reward-punishment idea of providence. We have seen already that Jesus had challenged this idea in his healing work, now he challenged the idea with regard to natural tragedies and disasters, 'Acts of God'. They are not necessarily a punishment for evil doing.

His reply boils down to saying: 'Do you think either of these sets of casualties had done something to deserve it? Not a bit. If that had been the way of it you would all have "had it" long ago, and the way you are going you are all heading for disaster.'

Think about disasters in your papers today. The one thing we *do* understand is that we have to do something to help. As we help, things fall into place. If we stand back and ask 'Why?' it remains a blank.

Luke 13:6–9

Jesus here gives us an insight into what we might call 'God's problem'; what to do about an unfruitful tree using up good ground. Should one cut it down and plant another or should one take a bit more trouble and see if it can be made fruitful?

We know the problem too: One person says: 'Sell the old car; it's just eating up money.' The other says: 'I think it will be all right if I get the cylinders rebored.' Or else: 'Fire that man; he's useless.' 'No, with retraining we might use him in another department.'

God had faced this problem for 2,000 years with the Jews (if one can say such a thing to God, but then Jesus suggests it!). Time and again He had given them a new chance, sending yet another prophet to speak in His Name, yet they never seemed to 'bear fruit'. Now, Jesus implies, they are getting their last chance.

For men, and for nations, there *is* a last chance, for God can go on knocking at the door of the human heart for so long, but eventually people and nations must reap what they have sown.

The relationship of the person to God, and of the nation to God is not like taking sugar in tea. It is a matter of life and death. What does this mean for me? For the nation of which I am a part? God give me grace to act *now*.

Luke 13:10–17

Here is a man for whom it was too late: this president of
the synagogue. He is like a man living in a condemned
building, who regards the men coming to take him to a
new home as enemies. One day he will find it too late to
have a dignified flitting! So it is with this religious leader.
His 'old time religion' is good enough for him, and he
sees Jesus as a threat to his familiar structure. He could not
see that this was his last chance to leave the collapsing
edifice, and to open out into a new religion of love, healing
and liberation.

In some ways we find religious leaders today like him.
Their concern is to patch up the old church structure, and
so they feel threatened by movements which go out to
contact the suffering masses of humanity. Sometimes it is
too late to patch up the old structure, because God has
moved on. One of the sure signs of decay is when people
get het up over the wrong things, like the president of that
synagogue. In the midst of the trouble in Northern Ireland
a minister said that ten years earlier the thing which had
really moved the Protestant conscience was some issue
about Sabbath observance, or betting shops. They had not
cared about the issues which were building up to disaster.
Now they wonder what they were *doing* all that time.

So, Jesus moved on leaving the man in his crumbling
synagogue. By the way, we would have said the woman
had arthritis, and we have seen people crippled by it,
healed. I remember one woman who had to be carried
into the house, going home and dancing the twist to prove
to her husband that she was healed. Over the next nine
years she never went back, though she had one or two
lesser attacks.

Luke 13:34–5

So, apparently, it *is* too late for Jerusalem. We must study these words carefully: God's Will, which is to say: 'What God wanted to do', was to gather this city as a hen gathers her chicks. What a tender, loving picture that is! 'But you would not let me.'

Yet even though it is too late, God does not wash His Hands of the city. In Jesus we see that He heads right for the centre of the coming disaster, and sets up there the sign of His Heartbreak: the Cross. Eventually Jerusalem would have to acknowledge Jesus, and so will every city. For some it will be a welcome relief, and a vindication of all they have lived for, whereas for others it will be a ghastly experience showing up wasted lives, and hidden corruption.

It is one thing to hear young people making sweeping condemnations of society, but it is another to see a great man weeping with loving grief over his nation. Jesus wept at the thought of Jerusalem, and over Edinburgh? London? Washington? Moscow? Can you go up a hill overlooking your town or city, look down on it, and try to see it from God's point of view?

Think of the succession of prophets (spokesmen) who have tried to teach the Jesus way. How have they been received? Look at the churches. Jesus said the Temple had been forsaken by God. It had remained static while God had moved on. Could the same be true of the church?

Introduction

Two rich men, some poor men, a beggarman go to make up our readings this week, and the thief is not all that far away either!

Each of these readings poses, in one way or the other, the question 'What is worthwhile in life?' Anybody who has looked death in the face knows that you get a very different idea as to what is important and what is not. One lesson is that possessions mean little, and what you *know* means a lot. That is why, as we draw nearer to the Cross, we have to start asking some really searching questions about life.

Some people seem to think that asking questions is a sign of a lack of faith, but this is wrong. There are two reasons for asking questions: one is that what you already know leads you on to want to know more. The second reason is that you are looking for an excuse to avoid the implications of a truth you know. If you find you are wanting to ask questions, having read this far, settle in your mind which of these reasons lies at the back of your mind, and if you are really wanting to know, do not hesitate to be fearless and far-reaching in your questioning.

No one minister or expert can answer all your questions. Nobody can hand you your faith on a plate. But your questions are signposts which will lead you to work out your own faith, so follow them.

'*Seek and you shall find*', said Jesus.

Luke 18:18–27

Remember, as you read this story, that the Jews tended to look on wealth as a sign of God's favour, and on poverty as a sign of His disfavour. That was another aspect of the reward-punishment idea of providence which we have noticed several times in our readings. In this case also, Jesus takes quite another view.

The first thing we notice is that Jesus did not like people bandying about words like 'good'. However, he took the man back to the ABC of religion, and the man was able to say in all good conscience that he had kept the commands. He must have been some man if he could look into the face of Jesus and say that! Yet he obviously felt a lack still, and knew that something was wrong, even though he had never blotted his copy-book.

St Mark tells us that Jesus looked at him and his heart warmed to him (Mark 10:21). This man was no sham, but the genuine article. His very feeling that something was lacking was a sign of grace. So Jesus came back with his shattering answer. Poor rich man! Yet how could he have become part of that group if he had wealth, servants and so on, while the fishermen and others were living rough? He might have become another rich supporter on the outside, but a man of that quality needed to be on the inside, and to come in he would have to come in as an equal.

Jesus' comments on the effects of wealth run clean counter to their usual ideas, and they are amazed. But Jesus, with wry humour, comments that God's power is so great that it is even possible for a rich man to be salvaged.

Jesus knew too much about poverty to wish that on people. Simplicity, sharing and sufficiency is the aim. The Christian needs *equipment* with which to serve his Lord, but not possessions, wealth, treasure. 'Seek ever to have less rather than more', said Thomas a Kempis.

What is hindering us from living more simply and communally?

Luke 18:28–34

Now it is Peter's turn to be taken aback. He and the others seem to have been still thinking of reaping an earthly reward for having followed Jesus. 'When Jesus becomes king . . .' how often they must have said that! Then they would know that it had been worth all this traipsing round the countryside.

One finds the same today. It often looks like a sacrifice when we begin to follow Jesus:

> a man leaves industry, and goes into the ministry on a much lower pay;
>
> a girl goes in for nursing with long, unsocial hours, instead of taking a better paid job,
>
> Sunday School teachers give up evenings for training and opportunities to go away at week-ends.

All these *look* like sacrifices, but later you are glad you did it, in fact it is these things which make sense of your life, not the things you gave up.

If you have helped somebody to know God, you have a deeper relationship with that person than with any mere blood-relation. Over the years the Christian finds a great number of 'new relations' in God, just as Jesus says.

The rat-race we 'give up' erects barriers between people, and cuts us off more and more. The more we 'succeed', the more isolated we become. In the rat-race we must always be on our guard against those trying to overtake us, and watching for the weakness in the man above us. But the Love of Jesus sets us free from all that, and gives us 'relations' all over the world!

As with Peter, we carry bits of the old outlook into our new life, and it spoils our joy. If we, like him at that time, are still thinking of 'our sacrifices' as bargaining counters which we hope to trade in later for 'good luck' then we have a lot to learn. We need no reward for discovering the Love of God!

Luke 18:35–43

By now Jesus had come to Jericho, about 20 miles from Jerusalem, one of the oldest inhabited sites on earth. It lies down in the Jordan valley, well below sea-level, and from it the road winds up to Jerusalem through rocky mountains, a long, hard walk in blistering heat.

The beggar at the gate is given a name in St Mark's Gospel: Bar Timaeus, or Son of Timaeus. We take it that Mark gave the name because it was one that was recognisable to the people for whom he wrote, so he must have become a well-known figure later.

We know from the history books that there were thousands of blind beggars in Palestine at that time, yet Jesus did not cure them all. It was Bartimaeus's determination which led to his healing. Shouting 'Son of David' was a dangerous thing to do, for it was a title for the long-awaited messiah. It was the sort of thing the police informers were watching for, and Jesus could not ignore it. The blind man's persistence reminds us of the story in Luke 11:5–10. So he is healed, and he follows Jesus, one of the few who are recorded as doing so after being healed.

In the experience of healing today, this rings true. It is people who seek for healing and will not be put off who find help. Those who need to be persuaded to have their names put on a prayer-list are not likely to find much help. The sad thing is that even after a life-time of reading the Gospels, most church people will not send for Jesus' representatives and ask for prayer. They may pray vaguely, and hope for the best. But the Bible tells us to send for the elders of the church (James 5), and it does lie with the sick person to insist on getting the Lord's blessing. If you are ill it is up to you to be like Bartimaeus, and *insist*. Do not wait for somebody to ask you: 'Would you like prayer?'

Luke 19:1–10

Now another story about that visit to Jericho, and once again the name of the person concerned is given. There is a tradition that Zacchaeus later became a friend of Peter's, and a bishop.

This undersized rich man had no claim to goodness to compare with the rich man we read about earlier. In fact he must have been a rogue to hold down a job like that. Yet, even in the strangest people you find some fragment of goodness left, some spark of 'soul' not quite killed off. You would find that in some unexpected people around you too. However, when Jesus stopped and invited himself to be the guest of such a man, he must have made himself very unpopular with the crowd. After all, they had suffered the depredations of this man and his staff fleecing them on behalf of the hated Roman occupation army. There were plenty of decent church folk he could have stayed with, why pick a rotten traitor like that?

It was this criticism which stopped Zacchaeus in his tracks. He saw that he was going to have to *do* something drastic to defend his new-found friend, and to justify his action. So he did what the other rich man could not do. The bad man did what the good man could not! He would have been ruined by making such a gesture, but he had seen enough of life to know that one healthy relationship was worth all the doubtful friends and the money he had accumulated.

Jesus' comment in verse 10 is one we have forgotten too often. The church's job is not to sit waiting for people to come, but to go out to seek and save the lost. If you are a church person, ask yourself how much is your Christianity a matter of activities inside the church, and how much is it a matter of going out to the unexpected places to get alongside people like Zacchaeus?

Introduction

Now we turn aside to look at some of the best loved words of Jesus, words which we recognize as linking up with the 23rd Psalm. St John tells us that it was winter when he said these things in the Temple, so we assume that he reached Jerusalem in the winter, said these words, and then withdrew to the safety of Transjordan, to await Passover.

In these words we are very conscious that Jesus is talking about the past and the future. He looks back to the prophecies of the Old Testament, to the sacrificial system of the past, and Israel's long tradition of shepherds or kings. He looks forward to his own death, which he knows is very close now, and beyond death too. And surely, these words come through as words which were meant, not just for the few who heard them then, but for the millions who would follow him in the centuries to follow.

As you read these words, alter them slightly to personal- ize them, so that the Lord is speaking them to *you*. This is what the Psalmist did when he wrote 'The Lord is *my* Shepherd...'.

John 10:1–5

Palestinian shepherds were, and probably still are, different
from British ones, and it makes this passage a lot clearer
when you know the difference. H. V. Morton describes a
scene in Palestine, in which he watched two shepherds who
had herded their flocks in a cave overnight. In the
morning each shepherd stood some distance back from the
cave and began a strange high-pitched chant, to which
the sheep responded by gathering round their respective
shepherds. Then each man set off, his flock following him.
There was no need of dogs, for there was no chasing. The
sheep followed the shepherd because there was a caring
relationship in which each was known by name.

With that in mind we see what Jesus meant. We know to
our cost that there are many ways of gaining control over
the flock; by working up mass hysteria, especially against
some other racial group; by brain-washing; by misusing
education; and so on. Jesus had refused these ways, as we
saw in his Temptations.

The other 'saviours' often have more, short-lived success,
but disaster always follows. Even the church has at times
resorted to the world's ways of gaining control of people,
and so has become yet another 'thief and robber'. For us,
the only way is the way Jesus took, the way of the Cross.
Each person must be won individually, a costly process.

Do we still think that there might be star preachers who
would bring people in 'en masse', and save us the trouble?
Are the churches empty because the masses do not hear
the authentic, caring voice of the Good Shepherd?

John 10:7–10

At the first reading it would seem as if the picture has changed from 'the shepherd' to 'the door', but in fact the picture remains the same, for in Palestine the shepherd slept across the entrance to the cave or fold, so that he was actually the door himself. It was *his body* which kept out prowlers, and he would protect the flock with his life.

So Jesus is saying that it is he himself who is the door providing protection, a way into the safety of the fold, and a way out to the pastures on the hills. It is through Jesus that we find our way *into* the fold of God's Love, and through Him we also move *out* into an awareness of spiritual things, the wider world of the Kingdom of God. Many people today are trying to find this through drugs, through exotic forms of religion and through the occult, and some do indeed seem to have found something, but experience shows that these 'doors' are very dangerous, 'thieves and robbers' abound in this area, and one is better to concentrate on him who is The Door.

As we trust in him, and follow him in loving service, the 'other world' becomes more real to us, and we become surer of the eternal things. We often find that we have discovered some of the strange things which people seek through the other 'doors', but if so, then it is because The Lord has revealed to us what we have the spiritual maturity to handle. For a spiritually immature person to discover psychic power is like giving a child a high-powered motor-bike.

Following Jesus means that you will discover 'life in all its fullness', the inner security of knowing that you are in God's Fold, and that you have a shepherd who cares, and leads, and also an expanding awareness of life, as door after door opens up on new truth and glory.

Be still for a moment. Allow the Lord to speak these words to you personally, especially those last words, about having life in all its fullness.

John 10:14–18

If you look up Ezekiel chapter 34 you will see why the
Jews thought Jesus was guilty of terrible blasphemy. The
Prophet (that word means 'spokesman' not 'fortune-
teller'!) speaking in God's name had said that God Himself
would come as the true Shepherd, and here was Jesus
saying 'I am the Good Shepherd'. It was a direct claim to
be fulfilling that prophecy.

But like the shepherd who lays down his life for the
flock, Jesus knew the cost. His picture of 'shepherding' was
not a pretty, romantic one! He was not going to his death as
a poor, persecuted victim. He knew just what he was doing.

Why should he die? Here is a simple pointer: if one
person wrongs another, then, before there can be reconciliation, the wrong must be faced. The one who is in the
wrong must say something like: 'My God, I never realized
how much I hurt you.' Once that has been said, there can
be AT-ONE-MENT, atonement. So, if there was to be at-one-
ment between God and man, God had to set before us the
plain sign of how man has hurt God, so that you and I
can come to the point of saying: 'My God, I never realized
how much I hurt you.'

Jesus does not ask for our pity, but he does ask us to face
up to our sin, our private sin, and our part in the sin of
humanity. Men of all religions have had a deep feeling
that somehow blood must be shed before reconciliation can
take place, and so there have always been sacrificial
systems, often explained in quite revolting terms. But the
fundamental truth is there, all the same, and now Jesus is
going to take on himself the function of all those victims of
sacrifice, human and animal, and in his own death make
possible reconciliation, atonement, between God and man,
between your Father and you. It is not a sacrifice to
placate a God who rejects you in anger, but it is, as Paul
says in Romans 5, the proof of God's Love for us: '*I love
you till it hurts like this*'.

John 10:22–31

It is good to learn verses 27–29 by heart. They will stand you in good stead when you come into 'The Valley of the Shadow of Death.' We and our loved ones must all pass through it sooner or later, and when that time comes, it is essential to have God's Promises deeply engrained into our minds.

Here we have the assurance that the life which Jesus gives us is eternal. That word does not really mean everlasting, it means rather a higher quality of life which transcends death. As we share more in his life on earth, we share more in his victory over death. As we learn to listen to The Good Shepherd day by day in the small things of life, we will be able to hear His familiar tones coming through the darkness, and then we can walk without fear.

We do not need proofs of survival, although we often find them. Rather we come to know this personal relationship with the Lord, and then we can say, with St Paul: 'I am confident that there is nothing in life or in death that can separate us from the love of God which is in Jesus Christ Our Lord.' (Romans 8:38–9).

When we walk with the Good Shepherd like this, we do not need fortune-tellers either, for we know that He has already gone into the future and has prepared the way for us. We do not need to know the future when we know that the Good Shepherd is leading us into it. All we have to do is to learn to walk more closely with him. Now take a fresh look at Psalm 23, and think of its meaning for you in your situation today. And try to learn those verses 27–29 by heart.

G

Introduction

Now at last the time has come for the final round. We have missed out the story of Lazarus, which, John tells us, happened a week or two earlier, and had been 'the last straw' for the religious authorities.

We call this week *Holy Week*, and it begins with Palm Sunday and ends with Easter Sunday. There is a traditional order of events, although, naturally, experts disagree over a number of points. But our readings this week cover the traditional first four days of the week, Sunday–Wednesday.

The point was that it was the week when pilgrims from all over the world converged on Jerusalem to celebrate the Passover. Historians have calculated that about a million people would be gathered around this little hill-top town, and then, as now, the authorities expected trouble. After all it was a celebration which looked back to the liberation from Egypt, as we read in the story of Exodus, and it was a looking-forward to a greater liberation, and for Jews of Jesus' time that meant mostly liberation from Rome. Then as now, political and nationalistic feelings ran high in Jerusalem at Passover time.

With so many people around it was hard to keep an eye on everybody, even with the very efficient secret police system they had then! That was why Jesus could slip away unseen and be lost in the milling crowds. We will see that he played this card very cleverly.

The authorities would have liked to liquidate him with no fuss, and they were experts at that game! They knew perhaps better than his supporters, that now was the time for Jesus to stake his claim to the throne as God's Messiah or else to slip back into obscurity. The crunch had come.

Luke 19:28–44

We call this Palm Sunday, the day when the city gave
Jesus a royal welcome, literally. They accepted Jesus as
Messiah, and he accepted their welcome. To understand
this better, it helps to know that in the days before radios,
one had to have ways of letting people know from a
distance what your intentions were. So if a king ap-
proached a city on an ass, they they knew he was coming
in peace, but if he came on a war-horse, they knew what
to expect! So Jesus' cards were on the table for all to see.

In verse 30 we read of how he had previously arranged
for the donkey to be ready, and had fixed a password. He
had to keep even his disciples guessing if he were to keep
one step ahead of the men who were out to get him. It was
a clever move, for the authorities would not dare to risk
serious trouble, so they had to allow this demonstration to
go on while they fumed. In vain they asked him to turn it
down a bit. His reply was a picturesque way of saying that
the truth was so obvious that even stones could see it,
surely. In the circumstances silent men would be as
unnatural as singing stones.

Yet he knew that in spite of the joyful singing of
favourite hymns, deep down in their hearts they wanted
another sort of deliverer. When the crunch came, the
crowd would not be there to back him. Eventually they
would support a man who took to the sword to set them
free, they would follow him and be massacred. So he wept,
even in the midst of the jubilation.

How about us, and our hymn-singing? It is so easy to
sing hymns about Jesus being Lord, but we do so little to
work out what it means in terms of the life of our city
today. Does God weep over us, saying: 'If only you had
known?' The fact of knowing the right hymns, and going
through the appropriate rituals only makes it sadder if we
miss the point, and head for disaster.

Luke 19:45–48

(St John gives us a longer account, but places it near the beginning of Jesus' ministry.)

The cleansing of the Temple we call this, and we remember it on the Monday of Holy Week. To imagine the scene, think of a playground with an arcade running round the outside, and a large complex of buildings towards one end. This courtyard was intended as the place where anybody could come to hear God's Law explained, and to hear about the belief that there is but *one* God, who requires justice and goodness.

Instead it had become the place where pilgrims were fleeced. They were not allowed to bring coins with the emperor's head into the Temple itself, so they had to change them here for Temple coinage, losing on the deal. They had to buy lambs or doves for sacrifice, and high prices were charged. The priests made a fortune from this racket, and it was the centre of the tourist trade, an economic necessity for the city.

The new 'King' would be expected to make some symbolic gesture that would express the 'line' he was going to take. They were expecting it to be some anti-Roman gesture. Imagine their horror, then, when the 'King' began by upsetting this profitable racket in the Temple. Matthew tells us that he went on to welcome the sick, the children and the beggars into the Temple, and the children began to dance round singing the bits of hymns they had picked up. The Temple was being used the way God was wanting it, for once.

If Jesus walked into our capital today, he might not begin by attacking atheists, communists, capitalists, or whatever the pet enemy happened to be. He might begin by attacking the churches.

We want God to solve the world's problems by attacking somebody else. He begins by cleaning up His People. Are we ready to accept that?

Luke 21:1–19

Doom! Jesus is back in the Temple, but they are not there to welcome and crown him. They are there with trick questions, out to trap him into an indictable offence. Chapter 20 tells of the cut and thrust of debate, but it would take too long to go into that.

At the end of the day, Jesus slipped away into the crowd. The verdict '*too late*' is now final. There is only one way ahead, a cross for Jesus, and ruin for the city.

His prediction of the future is a grim one. In many ways it is only too true to experience. Forty years later the city was destroyed, wars and horrors have been our lot ever since. In other ways it is puzzling, but it makes it easier to understand if you realize that the men who wrote down Jesus' various sayings on this subject, expected that the ruin of Jerusalem and the 'end of the world' would be much the same thing. They grouped together things Jesus said, but looking back we see that some of the sayings refer to the destruction of Jerusalem, and they were fulfilled to the letter. Other things he said are still working out. In Matthew's Gospel the same speech ends with the phrase: 'This Gospel of the Kingdom must be preached throughout the earth as a witness to all nations, then the end will come.' We have to finish *our* job of world mission before 'The End' can come.

Talking about 'The End', further on, verses 25–26 could be taken to refer to a nuclear explosion. Is there anything here to support the belief that life on this planet will slowly get better and better until it is Utopia? Why do people say that it shakes their faith when they see war and all that Jesus predicted?

The Christian's vocation is to remain faithful to the end, and not to be put off by the tragic results of man's rebellion against God, and the continuing rejection of the reign of Jesus.

End on a positive note by holding on to verse 19.

Mark 14:1–11

After yesterday's shattering reading, we come to a very different scene: Jesus spending the day quietly with friends. We usually take it that the woman referred to is the Mary about whom we read in Week 13 Day 3 (Luke 10:38–42).

The priests had not anointed Jesus as king in Jerusalem, but one follower now gives him his royal due. It was a beautiful gesture of loving faith set in the midst of the treachery, sin and misunderstanding around him. With the dark shadow of the cross looming over him, Jesus needed all the beauty and love his friends could give him.

The silly quarrel which broke out over it, is typical of what happens in a group when it is under strain. Everybody was over-wrought and ready to snap, so there was another quarrel. It seems to have been the last straw for Judas, who, St John tells us, was the treasurer of the group. There are many guesses as to why Judas betrayed Jesus, but they are only guesses, however interesting they may be. Bitter experience in the world today shows that when you have a group of twelve people under pressure in a police state, sooner or later one will turn informer. Many of our brethren in the church throughout the world know that only too well. Jesus' group was no exception.

But come back to Mary; there is a place in life for the extravagant gesture. We become so dull in our relationships and in our religion. Something crazy and costly is called for to break out of it. When did you last do something like this for somebody close to you? When did you last do something gloriously crazy for God's sake?

Introduction

This week we concentrate on one night, the Thursday before Jesus was executed. The Jews counted a day as running from sunset to sunset, the Romans thought of it as running from midnight, as we do, so it depends on how you see it whether it was Thursday or Friday.

In the background is the Passover supper, either that night, or due the next. If you have Jewish friends, you will know that this is still the big night of the year for them. As we have mentioned earlier, it celebrates the rescue of the Jewish slave-labourers from Egypt, and the deal God made with them: 'You keep the Ten Commandments, and I'll get you safely into the Promised land where you can begin a new life of your own.' You can read about it in Exodus 24. The details of the supper, which Jews still celebrate today, are in Exodus 12.

The first three Gospels and St Paul* all give us an account of what Jesus did with the bread and the wine. St John, however, never mentions sharing bread and wine, even though he spends five chapters, nearly a quarter of his Gospel on the Last Supper! He emphasizes 'Love one another', stressing that from now on his presence will be in the 'body' of his followers and not in the body of Jesus of Nazareth.

To our shame, Christians have argued and fought about what Jesus meant. We have even killed one another over it. How stupid can you get? Call it Communion, call it Mass, celebrate it in an upstairs room simply or with music and ritual in a cathedral, it does not matter. It is Jesus saying *Here I am, take me. Love one another, be one in me.*

Let us get on with it.

*See I Corinthians 11–23.

Mark 14:12–21

We begin by seeing that Jesus was still taking careful precautions to avoid being 'disposed of' quietly. He had arranged to borrow a room, and only he knew where. He kept Judas beside him, and gave the others no address, so that Judas would not know till he got there.

Jews normally ate dinner lying on low divans, each man leaning on his left elbow. Most likely there would be four divans around a low table, and three or four men on each. To judge by John 13:21–30 it would seem that John was lying to the front of Jesus, and Judas behind, with Peter near enough to be able to whisper to John, John to Jesus, and Jesus to Judas.

John also tells us that Jesus offered a piece of bread dipped in gravy, a sign of special friendship, to Judas. Apart from that appeal to the best in Judas he made no attempt to stop Judas going about his dark business. The last verse of our reading is an expression of *grief* over Judas which is rather lost in English; the Authorized Version, which has 'Woe to that man...', misses the mark by a mile.

This sums up God's way of dealing with man. We are not prevented from doing wrong, but in the long run it is fitted into a plan for good, even though we have to bear responsibility for the wrong. God may weep over us, as Jesus over Judas, but we remain free to do the wrong we have planned.

In many ways, the above picture of the Last Supper is unlike some of the famous pictures of it, in which Jesus is shown seated, Western fashion. But if you think it over, the story makes more sense when you picture it in the way it would have been, with thirteen working men lying round the table, having dinner in an upper room.

John 13: 1–17, 31–38

It was usual to have a slave to wash the feet of guests, because filthy streets, sandals and long walks added up to it being a very necessary but unpleasant job. When no slave appeared, and none of the Twelve was going to do the needful, Jesus himself 'took his jacket off', dressed like a slave, and did the dirty job. Peter found this humility unbearable, but had to submit in the end.

Jesus told us to carry on doing this, and some Christians have turned this into a ritual itself. Nearer to the spirit of obedience to Jesus' command, was the Boys' Brigade officer who, at the end of a B.B. camp, read this passage, with the comment: 'We've not washed each other's feet, but we've cleaned the toilets for each other.'

The humility of Jesus sprang from the fact that he was 'sure of himself' in the right way. The insecure person, unsure of himself, is afraid of humiliation, but Jesus, 'knowing that he came from God and was returning to God', was able to stoop humbly. Notice too, that at that moment when he was so aware of who he was and what he was, he did not preach a sermon, he took a towel. What has that to tell us about ourselves?

Finally we note his New Commandment. This new sort of *Love* was to be the hall-mark of the Church. His New Command was not: 'Be good' or even 'Go to Church', but 'Love each other.' Being a Christian is to do with being together in the love of Christ; you cannot be a Christian on your own. But Jesus was no starry-eyed idealist, for with that sublime command still echoing, he went on to speak of the weakness of his strongest disciple. His is a love that takes our weaknesses into account, as we must take each other's weaknesses into account, not idealising one another. How well do we carry out this command?

Mark 14:22–25

Still today, when Jews gather for their Passover meal, there is a ritual in which the youngest boy asks the meaning of the bread, wine, herbs etc. The father gives the ritual answer linking them with the deliverance from Egypt, and the Covenant which God made with His people Israel.

But at this supper, when the question was asked, Jesus did not give the ritual answer; he gave a new one, linking the bread with his body which was soon to be broken, and the wine with a new Covenant which God would make with mankind. As Moses had 'signed in God's Name' with the blood of sacrifices, so this new deal would be 'signed in blood'—the blood of Jesus.

Each of the first three Gospels, and St Paul whose account is the earliest, has the same outline, even if there are differences in detail.

'This bread and wine is ME, flesh and blood.

I break this bread as my body will be broken for you.
Share it and you become one body in me.
Eat it, it becomes part of you, and I will live in you and through you.

This Cup is the New Agreement which God makes with man.
I sign it in my own life-blood.
Share it and you are bound to God and to each other.
Drink it, and be filled with my life.'

That Table stretches down the centuries, and still the bread and wine pass from hand to hand, and you are asked to take your place, receiving God's love from others, passing it on to others, giving expression to that love which Jesus said was to be our hall-mark. There are many versions of this 'Sharing',* and as you grow in faith you will see new meaning in it all the time, for this is the central act of the Christian life.

*That is what the word for 'Communion' means.

Mark 14:32–52

This is a terrible glimpse into the agony that Jesus endured. Already we have seen signs of it mounting up: as he walked on alone, as he wept over the city, and so on. Now the curtain is pulled right back, and we look at a human being at the limit of his endurance through anguish. Luke tells us that he 'sweated blood', and Mark says that he *threw* himself on the ground. It all points to an extremity of suffering at which it is almost indecent to look.

Yet even if we must keep silent in the face of such a scene, perhaps we can venture to say that it was not just the fear of crucifixion which lay behind all this. Being human, that would have been one element, but only one. He says that it was an overwhelming horror of darkness. He was facing all the evil and wickedness in the world, and 'the powers of darkness' in their nightmarish power faced him.

In the midst of the horror of the trenches in the 1914 war, Studdart Kennedy wrote:

> 'The sorrows of God must be 'ard to bear
> If 'e really 'as love in his heart,
> And the 'ardest part in the world to play
> Must surely be God's part.'

Jesus was 'playing God's part' in earnest, and even he felt that it was too much for him. Only after a terrible struggle did he go on with it. As we read earlier in John 13, 'Now he was to show the full extent of his love', and it was a love tortured by the way we humans live. This is an aspect of God's love which few people realize, even though he showed it to us so clearly.

By the time we come to verse 48, Jesus is in command again, his usual self, in control of the situation.

Verses 51–2 sit oddly here, are they in fact St Mark saying: 'That was me, I was there. I saw it'?

Introduction

This week we see Jesus on trial for his life. St John gives us
the fullest account of the trial, and we gather that he
actually watched it from inside the palace. His Gospel
comments that he was known there; perhaps he had a fish
contract? We will read the shorter account in St Mark's
Gospel, but the notes will keep an eye on what St John
tells us.

Three of the main characters in the story are known
outside the Bible altogether, and this reminds us that we
are dealing with historical people who were alive and able
to protest if necessary when these stories were circulating.

The first is Caiaphas: son-in-law of the old, deposed
high-priest Annas. These priestly aristocrats were the real
rulers of the Jews. They trod a tricky path, with one eye on
pleasing the Roman conquerors, and the other on Jewish
religious extremists. They had to be a clever, ruthless lot.

Then we have Pontius Pilate: Roman Governor, mar-
ried to an Emperor's grand-daughter, appointed in AD 26,
dismissed from the post in AD 36 (Caiaphas lost his job in
the same upset.) He was a hard and ruthless man, who
eventually overdid it, so it is interesting to see him
squirming as he faces Jesus of Nazareth.

Finally we have King Herod: son of the Herod who
ruled when Jesus was born, brought up in Rome, more
Greek than Jewish, never really accepted by the Jews as
their king, for he was only partly Jewish, and not of
David's line. Like all his family he was treacherous, wily
and ruthless, but basically weak.

Here then is the historical setting for the trial, a
reminder that our story does not take place in a 'once
upon a time' world, but in the real world we know, with
characters we can recognize in terms of today's rulers in
the world.

Mark 14:53–65

When the Council, the Sanhedrin, met, it gathered in a horseshoe shape, with the juniors at each end, and the High Priest in the centre. The law required that all trials should take place by daylight, that all evidence had to agree word for word, and if the death-sentence was involved, the verdict had to be unanimous, and not executed until 24 hours later, just in case somebody changed his mind.

These were enlightened, humane laws, but Caiaphas could not wait. Jesus had to be out of the way by the time the Galilaean mob came into town. So he pushed the trial through illegally, and Jesus was within his rights to refuse to answer.

Caiaphas wanted to get Jesus on a political charge. Jesus wanted Caiaphas and the court to make up their minds on the religious issue: *Is Jesus the Messiah or not?* The two men faced each other, but Caiaphas was getting nowhere on his line. Finally, as dawn drew near, he did what he had no right to do: he asked the prisoner to incriminate himself. This was what Jesus was waiting for, and this time he answered clearly. The Council then had to decide either to accept Jesus, which would have upset their whole religious and social system, or reject him as a blasphemer. The verdict was a foregone conclusion, but not unanimous.

They had looked at Jesus; he did not represent God as they understood God, so they had to get rid of him. So it was that the leaders of the highest religion which the world knew, rejected God's Own Word made flesh. Some of the worst atrocities in history have been committed in the same way, by religious men who thought they were doing right. As in this case, they cause more harm than sinners, and their sin is all the worse, because they should have known better. '*They*'? Perhaps it should be '*us*'? Even good religion, when poisoned by human pride, can be terribly destructive, so let us search our own hearts.

Mark 14:66–72

Mark shows us the scene from outside the palace, with Peter in the gateway warming himself. It must have taken courage to follow as far as that. However his northern accent attracts attention, and the mocking tone of the serving lass proves too much for Peter. In Luke 22:61 it says that 'the Lord turned and looked at Peter', so perhaps Peter could see the Lord being beaten up, and knew what would happen to a follower. So can we blame him for his third denial? No wonder he wept.

Think too, of the Temple police. In the garden at the arrest they had been scared of Jesus, afraid he would use the supernatural power they had seen at work healing people. They hesitated to grab such a man. Yet when they did take him and nothing happened they would feel ashamed of their fear. Then they would take it out on him all the more.

So we move on to a scene which the modern world knows only too well: police brutality. Yet each of those men was probably a decent man who, given five minutes with Jesus on his own would have got on well with him. Yet once the brutality began, they were all caught up in it.

Think of Peter, and of them, and realize that we do not know how we would react in that sort of situation. So many of those who commit atrocities, and of those who betray their beliefs, are decent men and women, who never thought they could sink so low. Rather than condemn them, we should say: 'Perhaps that could be me, God help me!'

Part of the crushing burden of sin which the Lord bore are these sins, in which we all share, and which arise from our inability to say 'no' to social pressure. He sorrows over decent people doing terrible things, just because 'everybody else is doing it'. How much of the evil in the world is like this? God forgive us.

Mark 15:1–5

The Jewish rulers found it humiliating that they were not permitted to carry out their own death sentence. They had to get it confirmed by the Governor; so now we find Jesus confronting Pilate. Once more we see that it is not Jesus who is 'on the spot', it is the man who is trying him. Jesus watches and waits while Pilate flounders about trying to decide what to do.

Anybody who has had to do with politics knows that there is seldom a clear black or white decision to make. So Pilate tries to balance it all up. One wrong step and all hell will be let loose, many will lose their lives, and he will lose his job. Even if he saved Jesus, the priests would probably 'get him' somehow. He feels that Jesus is not really a political menace, and yet saving Jesus may put the whole city at risk.

John tells us that what finally did it, was the priests playing their trump card, see John 19: 12, 'no friend of Caesar's'. That phrase had the same ominous ring about it then that 'enemy of the people' has in communist countries. It was a veiled threat he could not ignore. Matt. 27:24 tells us that he tried to wash his hands of the whole business, literally, but you cannot do that in life. Politicians have to choose their shades of grey; we are the mob who put them on the spot. Jesus took his place among the victims of human injustice, and we cannot wash our hands. All over the world there are men and women in prison, and tortured by people who know that they are innocent, and Jesus takes his place among them.

Let us face this ghastly reality, summed up in Jesus' condemnation and torture. Pray for politicians who have to choose between several evils. Pray for victims of injustice, and see God there amongst them all, loving both torturer and tortured, judge and victim, at the receiving end of all the suffering and evil.

Mark 15:6–20

It would seem as if there were other potential victims for crucifixion, among them a man called Bar-Abbas, which means Son of Abbas, and some old versions of the Gospels give him a first-name: Jesus. He had killed somebody in one of the risings, and was due for execution. From the Israeli point of view he was a hero, a patriot. From the Roman point of view he was a terrorist.

So the crowd is faced with two men called Jesus, and it has to choose. It is a fairly common practice in many countries for a prisoner to be released to mark great occasions, so now Pilate gives them their choice. The crowd would have sympathy for Jesus of Nazareth, as a good man, but when forced to choose between a man who told them to love their enemies and a man who had killed an enemy, their choice was obvious. Forced to choose between the way of violence and the way of love, would we not choose as they did? We may like touches of religion here and there in life, but when it comes to a real political situation we choose the man of violence rather than the man of peace.

Pilate's last hope of saving Jesus was gone. He probably hoped that the flogging would kill Jesus, as it killed many people, sparing him the worse agony of crucifixion, but Jesus survived it. Then followed another ordeal, the only coronation the world was to give its rightful king, an old cloak, a crown of thorns (they have 2-inch spikes out there), and you have the royal regalia.

Here we see another aspect of human sin, that men can enjoy cruelty. Not many of us have to face this aspect of evil, but Jesus had to taste evil in all its horror. This *is* humanity, surely he cannot go on loving us now? We become embittered and disillusioned at far less. Think of times when you have been really hurt by evil. But not even this can stop Jesus loving us, and the love of God is unbroken. Nobody is written off; God bears the sin of the world in Jesus.

Introduction

This week we read about the Cross, the gallows on which Jesus was executed.

Today girls wear a cross round their necks as a pretty decoration; what a travesty of the hideous gallows! We sing hymns about 'He died for me on Calvaree' as if it was all a lovely story, without really seeing how this atrocity links up with *my* life today.

So this week, make a special effort to get through the fancy wrappings with which we insulate the Cross, and deprive it of its power. Lay aside the pictures, the pat religious phrases culled from hymns and all the rest of it. Try to read the story in all its stark reality, trying to see what the link is between *you* and that execution.

First let us look at some historical background. It was standard practice in the Roman empire to crucify slaves and rebels. On one occasion when a man claiming to be the Messiah arrived near Jerusalem, the Romans defeated him and nailed up about 2,000 people. So it was nothing unusual, and Jesus must have seen it many times. It was so indecent, that well-mannered people did not mention the word, and some time later it was abolished as a form of punishment, for it offended even the callous Romans.

Our readings this week are going to be three different points of view of the Cross, Mark's, Luke's and John's and we will then go on to read John's account of the burial. So it is one event looked at from three points of view, rather than the three or four events that have made up other weeks. You will probably want to look up St Matthew's account too, just to complete the picture.

H

Mark 15:21–39

Roman regulations were that a criminal had to carry the cross-piece of his gallows by the longest route to the gallows hill, where the cross-piece was fixed to the upright, which was often permanent, and he was nailed or tied to the cross-piece.

The treatment Jesus had received had led to such loss of blood that he could not carry the heavy beam, so they conscripted a man to carry it for him.

A guild of women in the city used to offer drugged wine to victims, to dull the pain, but Jesus knew that the spiritual battle he was fighting called for a mind clear of drugs (verse 23).

That terrible cry recorded in verse 34 is shattering. It takes us back to Psalm 22, which Jesus must have known by heart. The mental agony of which we caught a glimpse in Gethsemane is now flooding back. You can do one of two things when you are hurt by somebody you love, you can bear it, accepting the pain, or you can wash your hands of the person who has hurt you. Jesus at this point was *bearing* the sin of humanity, refusing to be finished with us.

He had acted out God's love perfectly towards men, and their response had been: 'Crucify him.' So it would seem that the gulf between God and man was unbridgeable. Yet this cry in the darkness shows that Jesus is still on the man side of the gulf, going through hell. It was Hell. He knew it now. Jesus was still God-with-us, even in Hell.

A great minister, Tom Allan, once said: 'I can't understand how God Almighty could get himself into the position in which He could say *that*, but I do know that only one who has been through that can be my God.'

That love is over me, today, bearing my sin, loving me eternally. When I know that, a new love is born within me, a new relationship with God begins, and a life begins which death cannot destroy.... Then I know that he died for *me*.

Luke 23:26–47

Luke gives us four of Jesus' last sayings, and each one is another window into the inner mystery of God's Love.

In verse 28 we have 'Weep not for me...', reminding us that he is not asking for pity, rather he is trying to bring us to our senses in time.

In verse 34 we read of how he is still concerned for the soldiers, coarsened by their hard life, and probably half-drunk, doing their horrible duty. Theirs is the tragedy of mankind: we do not know what we are doing until it is too late. But from the bottom of the heap of the world's atrocities comes this plea for mercy for those who do these terrible things.

In verse 43 we see him still concerned for others. Most of us would have written the thief's cry off as delirium, yet Jesus sees something worth salvaging in this wreck. Pain makes us self-centred, yet Jesus is still thinking of others; what love! This calm assurance on the verge of death has been a comfort to countless people.

Luke refers to a 'loud cry', perhaps the cry we looked at in Mark 15:34, and then he tells us of Jesus' last prayer. It is a quotation from Psalm 31, and was (and still is) the good-night prayer of Jewish children, except that Jesus added his own word 'Abba', which you will remember is the family word for 'father'. So from the hellish darkness of forsakenness he has struggled through to the simplicity of a little child falling asleep. That is victory.

Love for God and love for man have remained unbroken by the ordeal. Loving trust has the last word, literally. The bridge between man at his worst and the perfect love of God was complete, and many of us who have experienced god-forsakenness have been able to pass over the Living Bridge into the experience of the Love of God.

John 19:17–30

John adds several touches of his own, and it is obvious that he was there, even if he avoids putting his own name in.

In verses 25–27 we see that Jesus was still concerned to follow up his Last Command: 'Love one another.' In the light of his cross we must all look on each other as his family.

Verse 28 is the only reference to physical pain. Those with war-time experience know that eventually it is thirst that becomes the all-consuming agony as the sun dries up the organs. This word gasped out is horribly true to life, and reminds us that Jesus was really human. Yet we must remember, too, that without some moisture he would not have been able to make his final words heard.

Isn't it strange that at the end it was a Roman soldier who made a kind gesture, offering him some of the sour wine which was issued to soldiers on this horrible duty? In this foreigner's offer of wine we catch a glimpse of the world-wide movement to come.

In verse 30 we have another word, and in Greek it *is* one word. Presumably it came just before the final prayer recorded in Luke. This word does not mean: 'It's all over.' It is the sort of word you might use when you had reached the top of a high mountain, or finished a difficult job. It is more like 'I've made it!'

We read earlier in John 13 that Jesus was 'going to show us the full extent of his love'. What greater love could there be than a love which is prepared to suffer like that, and still go on loving until the end? His work was finished, the embodiment of God's Love was complete.

Yet though *his* part was complete, mine is just beginning. If that is how God loves me, and how I hurt Him, then I must indeed 'weep for myself', as Jesus said. All that I am ashamed of, and all that I am proud of, must be crucified with Christ, so that a new life in me may be raised up. Out of that blood-shed, a new life is born.

John 19:31–42

So the religious leaders don't want their celebrations
defiled by having bodies, dead and dying on the gibbet.
How twisted can you get? The normal thing was to leave
the poor wretches lingering for days, but to satisfy their
religious principles, the victims were to be brutally finished
off, except that Jesus was found to be dead already.

There have always been those who thought that Jesus
just swooned on the cross, and revived in the cool tomb.
Such people cannot have seen men dying in the Middle-
East, in the scorching sun, the clouds of insects and the
swirling dust. Also, according to medical experts, the
'water' which John saw would have been clear fluid, which
shows that Jesus died, literally, of a broken heart. Jesus
was *dead*. They were quite clear on that.

The 'Joseph' mentioned is usually thought to have been
the 'rich young ruler' we read about in Luke 18:18. We
read about Nicodemus right at the beginning when we
looked at John 3. Their concern must have made them
marked men from then on, so they had found real courage
at last. It was really against regulations for Pilate to grant
their request, so it tells us something about him, that he
did.

These garden tombs can still be seen: caves carved out
of the hill-side, with massive stone doors which roll down
into position to block the entrance.

So Jesus' supporters turn away sadly thinking that Jesus
is just 'a thing of the past'. It seemed as if the evil in
mankind had been too much for him. People still make the
same mistake. But Jesus is not buried in empty churches,
confined to ancient rituals. He still has a way of
surprising people! Thank God!

Introduction

Resurrection, what does that word mean? It is something we have never experienced, and there has never been anything else like it, so we have to say that we do not know what it means. It is a long word to hide our ignorance. We know about 'resuscitation', either through the 'kiss of life' or through mechanical methods, but that is not 'resurrection'. The Gospels make it quite clear that Jesus after Easter was not just continuing his previous life, as Lazarus would have done. St Paul in I Corinthians 15 makes that clear too. It is not that the body was resuscitated.

Let us start with an open mind, then, clearing away any ideas which we may have gathered, in the Sunday School, for example. We are faced with a mystery, and the only proper attitude of mind is a respectful openness, ready to receive any glimpses of truth which dawn on us, but not expecting to get it all neatly tied up.

Two Gospels give us fairly detailed accounts of it: John's and Luke's. These men were not ignorant, superstitious peasants. By their writings we know them to have been educated men, able to hold their own in a sophisticated society. Both must have known quite clearly that what they wrote seemed contradictory if one accepted the current ideas of 'spiritual' and 'material'. They were both clearly aware that Jesus was neither a 'spirit' on the one hand, nor a resuscitated human on the other. Some parts of their stories suggest one, while some suggest the other, but they leave us bewildered. Perhaps the trouble is that the relationship between the spiritual and the material is not as simple as people think.

It they had been making it all up, then they would have made their stories fit their own ideas. They would have tried to make it more credible and acceptable to people then or now. Instead, they recorded a bewildering series of incidents, in which Jesus materializes and dematerializes. They leave us with an empty tomb, shrouded in mystery.

John 20: 1–9

We begin by looking at what John tells us. He begins by telling us about Mary; presumably the one who annointed Jesus' feet. If we compare this with Mark's account we find that Mary came to the tomb as one of a party of women in the first instance and that previously Jesus 'had cast seven devils out of her'. It seems that they were going to the tomb to anoint the body, as we would put flowers on the grave, before the heat of the day made the stench unbearable.

Mary's first reaction was that '*they*', the authorities, had removed the body, carrying their spite out to the last. Naturally she went and told the men, and John has the lovely story of how he and Peter ran together. He, being the younger, got there first, but as a sensitive person, he hesitated. Peter, typically, dashed right in. John comments that the linen wrappings were lying there, and the napkin which had been over his head was 'separated, infolded in one place'. That is what the Greek words actually say, but most English translations have a go at guessing what these words refer to. The most likely meaning is that the grave-clothes had just 'deflated' when the body of Jesus dematerialized, and were lying undisturbed, showing that the body had not been stolen.

John comments that he began to realize what had happened, whereas Peter was still just puzzled. As a whole, the friends of Jesus just could not take it in, and their bewilderment is registered in all the Gospels.

John 20:10–18

As Peter and John walk away, Mary is left alone, and we can imagine her state of mind! Those 'seven devils' would come sweeping back now that Jesus was dead, and she did not even have the dead body in a grave to turn to.

In her grief and despair she would hardly be aware of the figures in the cave. Mark says it was 'a young man', Luke says 'two men in shining clothes' while John says 'two angels'. Again, we are confused because we *think* we know what an angel is, and we do not. The Greek word means an *imperial messenger*, and we have no authorized picture of what angels look like. Mary must have been dimly aware of figures, and so she said 'two messengers'.

However, the 'messengers' were no use to her. Her whole being cried out for the Lord Himself, and yet she did not recognize him when he did speak. She thought that it was the gardener, and assumed that he had cleared the corpse of the gallows-bird out of his master's tomb. Mary offered to tidy it up, whatever he had done with it. A typical response for a woman!

Her next response was also typical: Jesus had to tell her not to cling to him...that is what the words mean. But how typical of Jesus is the fact that it was to Mary that he first appeared. His priorities are the priorities of need, and her need was greatest. But it must have gone against the grain for men brought up as Jews to have to record that a woman was the first witness, the first to bring the good news: 'The Lord is risen!' That was not made up for propaganda purposes!

John 20:19–23

Did the disciples make this story up as a deliberate lie? Were they suffering from mass hallucination? Let us face these two questions.

Firstly: Was it a lie? What had they to gain by saying that Jesus had appeared? It would mean that they would have to go on, taking the Jesus-line. They were putting their heads into the noose, or taking up the cross, by saying that. They had nothing to gain, and all to lose. To imagine that they had a week-end committee meeting and cooked up the Gospel, which they knew to be false, and then went out to convince the world of it at the cost of their own lives, just does not make sense. *They must have believed it themselves.*

Were they deluded? The only type of delusion known to us which could produce this effect is mass hypnotism by a very strong person, and to carry weight the victims would have to be suggestible people. Such people would not carry the conviction they did. They would not be the sort of people the Roman Empire would have to liquidate as a menace.

Remember too that what comes across is very different from the sort of messages we get at seances from 'granny on the other side'. Here are no sugary assurances about survival, but orders to get on with the job here on earth: marching orders. There is no wishful thinking here!

Something happened to turn that quarrelling group of men and women, who could not get the hang of what Jesus was saying, into a body of people who started a movement which still goes on today. For us too, to discover that Jesus is a Risen Lord, means that we face a challenge: '*I send you*'. We become people with a mission, which may cost life itself. There can be no wishful thinking for us either. But to be part of a fellowship in which the Risen Lord is real, is the one thing that makes sense of life.

John 20:24–29

Most of us feel for Thomas; he speaks for us. Yet Jesus did come to Thomas, and when we say the same thing, nothing happens. Perhaps the difference lies in the fact that Thomas had seen the crucifixion, and had been so shattered by it that only *seeing* those hands and feet could heal the spiritual wounds he had received.

When we wish for an experience like that, we must remember that the object of His coming was to allow us to discover the Love of God working through *us*. Later we will look at The Ascension, which marked the end of this type of experience. Many people ever since have had visions of Jesus, but that is something quite different.

It is John who stresses, in his letter, that for us the Love of God is to be experienced in our love for one another. Thomas did have an experience of the Love of God in a human and in a resurrection body, but that is not for us. We must find it in the work of His Spirit within people, and in ourselves.

We note, too, that Thomas was the first to realize who Jesus was, for he said: 'My Lord and my God.' This wounded figure *is God*. To look at Jesus and to say 'My God' was to start a new era. Can you look back on what you have read, then look up to him and say:

'*My Lord and My God*'?

Introduction

Last week we looked at the Easter story as recorded in St John's Gospel; this week we look at St Luke's account, and at the fragments in St Mark and St Matthew.

You will notice that it is not easy to piece them together so that they all fit perfectly. But remember that the people about whom we are reading, are men who had been shattered over that awful week-end when Jesus was executed, and then uplifted to heights of elation they could little have dreamed of. So as they looked back on it twenty to thirty years later, it is not surprising that details in their accounts varied. The differences show us that they were not trotting out a 'party line', but were telling things as they remembered them, or as they had been told.

If you want to read more about this in detail, you could get Frank Morrison's book *Who moved the stone?* He set out to write a book to prove that the resurrection did *not* happen, and found himself convinced by the evidence that it *did*. Reliable evidence usually does have variations, whereas if a number of witnesses come out with exactly the same story, one suspects collusion. So we are not put off when we read, for instance, that John only mentions one woman at the tomb, whereas the others mention several; we look rather for the element that is common to all.

It is worth emphasizing again that Faith does not mean that you ask no questions. Being afraid to question may indicate that you are afraid that the object of your faith may not bear the weight of even one puny human mind. Real faith seeks to come to grips with the facts, believing that there is an answer. Such a search for truth does have its painful stages, but what we discover is of more value than any preconceived ideas we lose in the process. What emerges is our own faith, and nobody else's.

Mark 16:1–8

St Mark's Gospel itself ends at verse 8 in the middle of a sentence: 'They were afraid of. . . .' We do not know why it ends like this, and many people later tried to put endings to it. Very old documents have different endings, and if you read from the New English Bible it gives you a selection. But let us confine ourselves to the bit that was actually St Mark's.

He tells us that it was the women who discovered the tomb empty. He does not suggest that the 'young man' who spoke to them was supernatural, and yet the women are afraid, whereas when we read St John's account, it was two 'angels' who spoke, and Mary practically ignored them! It is the strange sort of detail that leaves us wondering.

There is one detail here which is moving, and that is that a special message is sent to Peter. After all, it might not be very good news to Peter that the Lord was risen. He had denied Him, and would find it hard to face Him. So this special message of reassurance to Peter was a way of breaking it gently. It says here that the women did not say anything to anybody, yet John says that Mary of Magdala did do what the 'young man' told them. Perhaps the other women kept it to themselves at first.

However the bits of the story may fit together, it becomes clear that a woman, or women, find the empty tomb, and a being of some description deals with them. Remember that this tomb was only minutes from the city, and must have been public knowledge, as Frank Morrison points out. The story would never have stood up if, when the crowds had gone out to look, they had not found an empty tomb. One way or the other, that tomb was empty.

Luke 23: 55 56 and 24: 1–11

In Luke too we get the same drift. One or two details are different, but the message is the same. We have two men in dazzling clothes instead of one young man in white, and we have a fuller account of what was said by them. Whereas St Mark says that the women did not say anything to anybody, St Luke says that they told the eleven and the rest. However in verse 12 we have a detail which ties in with St John's account. Mary of Magdala is mentioned in them all, but only St John tells us the story about her at the tomb.

In verse 11 we get an insight into what the disciples thought. Their disbelief is understandable, especially when you remember that as Jews of their day and age, they would not have considered women as reliable beings, worth listening to. As we have seen already, the important place of women in this story would have made it all the more difficult for men of that time to swallow. If the disciples had been making it up they would not have given women such an important place.

But perhaps the phrase which comes out from this account is: '*Why seek the living among the dead?*' We continually make the mistake of looking for God among the 'dead' of this world, as if He were mostly a thing of the past. But just when people think that He is dead and buried, we find that He is there opening up a new future. Sometimes, like Russian communists, they *want* to think Him buried, a thing of the past, and are upset that the new generation is taking an interest in religion after all. Sometimes His followers weep over their empty churches, regretting that nobody seems to care any more, while He is bursting through in new ways they never think of, and therefore do not see. 'Why seek the living among the dead?'

Matthew 28:1–15

Matthew's version has quite a different slant. Nobody else mentions the soldiers, but Matthew makes a lot of this side of things. It has been noticed that a lot of the stories in Matthew's Gospel which are in his Gospel only, concern Jerusalem. He seems therefore to have had sources of information around the capital city. That would be where the stories of the soldiers fit in. Perhaps one of them was known to the church in Jerusalem later, and handed on his view of things.

What is difficult to sort out is that in this account it says specifically that the stone was rolled away while the women were present, whereas the other three all say that the stone was found already rolled away.

In verses 9–10 we find a story which ties in with the story we read about Mary of Magdala, only here it seems that the Lord appeared to all the women, whereas in St John's Gospel it is only to Mary.

Verses 11–15 give us a fascinating glimpse of what was going on in the world around them. Yet why *should* the disciples steal the body? All along we have noted that they had never been very quick at picking up what he had been saying, and were always quarrelling. We can see, too, that whereas this tendency appears in the earliest Gospel, St Mark's, the later Gospels tend to play it down a bit. So it would appear that since it went against the grain for the writers, they did not invent it. So it seems unlikely that suddenly they had:

> the *courage* to steal the body;
> the *wisdom* to think up a new, cross-centred religion;
> the *conviction* to carry their message through; and
> the *dishonesty* to perpetrate such a lie.

They must have believed in what they were saying, and whoever it was that emptied the tomb, it was not they.

Luke 24:13–42

This is a long story, and yet it is a pity to break it up. Read it as a story, and let it flow over you.

The main character in the first part is Cleophas. He has only appeared before as the father of one of the twelve, and as the husband of one of the Marys who were at the Cross, although in those cases we get the Greek form of his name, Alphaeus. Now he and another disciple are slipping away home quietly, for Jerusalem is a dangerous place for followers of Jesus.

Their despondency comes through clearly, and the reason is seen in verse 21: they are still hoping that Jesus is going to liberate the Jews from the Romans. They had not really listened to what Jesus was saying, and because God was not fulfilling *their* expectations they were in despair. Many of our dark moments are perhaps rooted in the same mistake.

In both parts of the story we have Jesus doing some Bible Study with the disciples, and in both parts he takes food, stressing that he is not a ghost, even though he materializes and dematerializes.

If we want to know that he is risen and in our midst, then we have these two pointers: Bible Study and the sharing of food, not necessarily in a formal way as we do at a Communion Service.

There are times for us, when 'our hearts burn within us' and the Bible takes on new meaning. Then we know that *He* is there. There are times too when we take the step which those two took, inviting a stranger into our homes, and we find that the Lord has come in to visit us.

It is from this story that we get the great Easter greeting:

> *The Lord is risen!*
> *He is risen indeed!*

As the reality of that dawns upon us, we can really begin to live the Christian life, knowing that death is defeated and that Jesus lives, and we too shall live.

Introduction

This week we look at the final story in St John's Gospel, and we look at what St Paul and St Peter said in other parts of the New Testament.

We look again at the prayer by an English saint, Richard of Chichester, which sums up our attitude as we read these stories:

'Lord Jesus,
     Merciful Friend, Redeemer and Brother,
Grant that we may see thee more clearly
               love thee more dearly
               and follow thee more nearly.'

Go over that prayer again and again as you read these stories, for we are not just asking whether a man who lived 2,000 years ago survived death or not.

We want to know if we too can know him.
We want to know if this was in fact God coming to our rescue.
We want to know if Jesus holds the answer to *our* defeats.
We want to know if his conquest of death is relevant to the fact that we too must die some day.

For many of us Jesus is a Living Lord, and we want to share that knowledge with you, and that prayer sums up the progress of the Christian life:

we come to know him as we study his Word,
then we come to love him,
then we want to live in the light of that love.

We do not start with living the Christian life, and then getting to know God. We begin by coming to love the Lord, and then the Christian life follows from that. So make this your prayer this week, adapting it to meet your need.

John 21:1–14

We remember that the disciples were real people, who had to earn a living. So in this story we see them back at work. It is typical of Jesus that he should do a menial job like this: getting breakfast ready for men on the night-shift. The Risen Lord remains 'down to earth'.

We note in this story yet again, that Jesus is fully materialized, having lit a fire and cooked breakfast. Yet we notice too that there is something different about him, and in this story, as in some of the others we have read, close friends are not sure at first who he is. It is a surprising point which we find in several of the stories, but we do not know why. ·

This story is important in that it stresses that he came to them in the cold light of morning, at their work, and not just in the Upper Room. This shows us that the Resurrection was not linked with some spiritualist-type activity. He did not come back as the result of some mystical or psychic exercise performed by men. He came back by his own decision.

Yet again we see that eating together is part of the Resurrection experience, even though it is breakfast this time and not supper. It is no wonder that Christian people the world over are trying to recover the practice of eating together, and not just attending services, taking perhaps a crumb of bread and a sip of wine. Christians should try to eat together regularly, and the common meal should be part of their life together.

J

John 21:15–25

This passage sounds like sickly sentimentality at first. But it takes on new meaning if you look at the footnotes in the New English Bible. The point is that there are a number of words in Greek for *love*, and two of them are used in this passage.

Agape is the first word used, as in the command *love God* and 'love one another as I have loved you'. It is a love which rises above likes and dislikes. There is nothing sentimental about this sort of love.

Phileia is the love which you have for a friend. They had yet another word for sex-love, *eros*, and that, of course, does not come into our reading here.

Now look at the passage again. Once Peter had boasted that even though everybody else denied Jesus, he never would. So Jesus asks him whether he still maintains that his love is better than everybody else's. Peter answers, using only the word for friendship. Seeing that Peter has avoided using the great word *agape*, Jesus asks him straight, no comparisons this time. Peter sticks to asserting that he is Jesus' friend. Then Jesus comes down to questioning even that, and *he* uses the friendship word this time. Peter is driven to throw himself on the Lord's understanding. 'You know I'm your friend.'

So Peter worked off his three-fold denial. It was a painful and necessary exercise, and by no means sloppy. Only after he had been through this confrontation could he set about the job that lay ahead, and with each question, the Lord gives Peter a bigger job to do. He is saying: 'Stop being morbid about your failure. Get on with the job. Think of the needs of others.'

Each account of the Resurrection ends on the note of *mission*. To know the Risen Christ means that we can never go back to the old pattern of life, but must face the world spreading the good news, loving and caring for people in the Name of the Good Shepherd.

Acts 10:34–43

Now we see Peter in action, obeying the Lord's command, and we read part of one of his sermons. It was a great occasion and marks a turning point in the church's life. Up to that point the converts had been Jews, but now we see Peter preaching to a Roman officer and his household. It is beginning to dawn on them that Jesus really meant what he said about 'the whole world' But there was a good deal of opposition at first within the church to 'going international' like this.

You will notice that once again Peter emphasized that Jesus ate and drank with them after the Resurrection. This earthy touch was part of the Gospel, but never popular. It went against all that they had been taught, as we saw earlier. It was bad enough saying that God had revealed Himself in an ordinary carpenter, it was even worse to suggest that God was to be seen in an executed criminal, and the final nonsense seemed to be this eating and drinking with them. But that is the way it was.

Perhaps we too try to avoid the earthiness of the Gospel by having Jesus in stained glass windows, surrounded with impressive rituals, barricaded behind masses of heavy books.

Peter's final note is on forgiveness. That was the Gospel that he, and we, are entitled to preach. We preach forgiveness because that is what we all need. One minister was asked why ministers were 'always on about sin'. His answer was that we ministers know that it is such a problem in our own lives. As forgiven people we proclaim forgiveness.

I Corinthians 15: 3–8

This is the final bit of evidence about the Resurrection that we shall look at. Yet, as far as we can work out, it was in writing long before anything else we have read. Paul was writing to the little church in Corinth, around AD 52, about twenty years after the event, and about twenty years before Mark wrote down his Gospel. Paul assumes that the people he was writing to knew the story well, and only reminds them of the highlights.

He mentions that the Lord appeared to Peter, or Cephas; it is the same name, just as 'Iain' is the Gaelic for 'John'. When we read Luke 24:34 this appearance was mentioned also, but we have no details about it. We wonder how it fits in with the story we read last week when Jesus asked Peter 'Lovest thou me?'

We would very much like to know the story of how Jesus appeared to over 500 at once, but we don't. However, notice that Paul knew that there were plenty of people around who could say 'I saw him'. He also mentions an appearance to James, presumably the 'brother of the Lord' mentioned in Galatians 1:19, who became the leader of the church in Jerusalem. We have no account of that either.

Look back over what we have read about the Risen Lord. Make up your own mind:

> Were the apostles deliberately lying?
> Were they suffering from hallucinations?
> Were they bearing witness to something that really happened?

Introduction

We have looked at the accounts of the Resurrection, and have tried to work out what happened. This week we look at what flowed from those events. We might have called this week 'So what?' The greatest test of whether there was *truth* in what was written lies in what they *did* about it. 'The proof of the pudding is in the eating', or, as Jesus said: 'By their fruits shall you know them.'

But before we go on, let us note one surprising omission. One would have expected a great fuss to have been made about relics of Jesus and places associated with him. We know that early in the church's life they made a great deal of the tombs and relics of the apostles, which shows that they acted as one would have expected. All the more surprising is it, then, when there is nothing of this for Jesus Himself. He was a living Lord, who needed no relics, no memorials.

Centuries later, when Christianity was beginning to be powerful in a worldly sense, an Empress demanded to know where the holy places in Jerusalem were, to fill in this surprising omission. She was duly given the information she had asked for, but seeing the Romans had razed the city and it had been rebuilt, it is not likely that the information she was given was all that reliable. Then the whole relic industry got going, with enough pieces of the 'true cross' to rebuild Jerusalem in wood!

Which all goes to show that those first Christians really knew a Risen Lord. If they had been carrying out a mass deception, they would hardly have overlooked such a lucrative item! The novel *The Robe* is very moving, but it misses the point that there was no sign of this type of thing. What followed from the Cross looked forward, not backwards.

Luke 24:44–49

The first part of St Luke's story of the Risen Christ we read two weeks ago. Now we come to the summary of what Jesus was saying to the disciples when he came back to them.

First of all he directed their thoughts to the Bible, that part of it which we call *The Old Testament*. Helping them to understand what had happened in the light of what was written, he was helping them to come to terms with what had seemed an unmitigated disaster.

Then, as we have seen already, he directed their thoughts outwards to the 'whole world'. They were to spread the Gospel to all nations, a seemingly impossible task for a group of comparatively poorly educated peasants, whose leader had been executed! No wonder he told them not to try it until they had received 'power from on high'.

The good news they have to spread, is that God's free pardon is extended to all men. That is the origin of the word 'Gospel', which is English for *Evangel*, which was the term used for the pardon sent to a man in exile or in prison saying that he could go home and take up life again as a free man.

But before reconciliation can take place between any two parties, one must face how badly he has wronged the other, and really *want* a new relationship. That is why the Gospel begins by pointing people to the Cross, saying: 'This is how you have hurt God.' When they seek forgiveness and a new relationship, then a new relationship is possible, and they are free to 'come home', with all past sins forgiven.

Jesus did not send them out saying 'Tell everybody to love one another.' That is what he says to those who have responded to the Gospel. Our job as Christians is first of all to point to the forgiveness of God.

Matthew 28:16–20

The ending of this Gospel is also on the note: GO! We may disagree with the way some Christians have gone about 'missions', but there is no doubt that the Christian is one who is *sent* with good news which he must spread everywhere.

In this passage we read that Jesus commanded baptism, and this is the passage which we usually read at baptisms. Jesus did not have babies, pink ribbons, fancy cakes and god-mothers in mind. What it meant in those days, and is coming back to mean in ours, is that when a person is going to become a Christian, he or she is to be dipped (that is what the word 'baptism' means) in water, as a symbol of washing away the old life, and being raised up to a new life. Paul said that it was being buried with Christ and raised together with him.

This new life would mean becoming part of a new family, the church, which centres in gathering at the Lord's Table, around which the new life of love grows up, and we experience the Holy Spirit's power working through our lives.

Very early in the life of the Church, people tended to come, not as individuals, but as families, including babies, and the whole household was baptized together. That is how baptism came to be done for babies, when it was not meant for them primarily. Many Christians today, called Baptists, only baptize believers who are old enough to confess their faith. Perhaps they are right.

But whatever we may discuss on that issue, let us end by taking to ourselves the great promise: *I am with you always*. That applies to you, today, wherever you may go. He has given you his Word, and he will never go back on it.

Philippians 2:5–11

Our reading today is part of a letter, written by St Paul in a prison cell somewhere about AD 53, probably about ten years before the Gospels as we know them began to be written.

Here we have the over-all picture of what we have read in detail, the whole story in one great sweep; from the heights of heaven, down to the depths of humiliation, suffering and death itself, and up again into the heights. It ends with the vision of all humanity . . . and of creatures beyond humanity, all shouting '*Jesus is Lord*'. Those words formed the first Christian creed, which later grew into the creeds as we know them. But in those days, just the words 'Jesus is Lord' meant that you were a Christian.

This picture of the final victory celebration is what keeps us going. Eventually the last straggler will be brought home, the last lost sheep returned to the fold. God's love cannot rest until that has happened, which is why we Christians cannot rest either until our mission is accomplished. Our mission is to express the love of God to every living creature. We have all known people who have tried to force their views of religion on everybody, and that has made the words 'mission' and 'missionary' dirty words for so many people. But we have to become part of God's outreach, and, like Jesus, seek to plumb the depths of this world's darkness in order to reach God's lost children, and bring them Home.

This is not always done most effectively by those who most readily use the word 'mission', but from now on you are a 'man with a mission in life', or 'a woman with a mission'. Life can never be meaningless again, once you accept *his* meaning for your life. Even the depths take on meaning, and we know that the victory celebrations lie ahead.

John 20: 30–31 and 21: 24–25

It looks as if John was going to end his Gospel at the end of chapter 20, but then felt that he just *had* to tell the story which makes up chapter 21, so his Gospel has two endings!

In 20:31 John speaks to *you* across the centuries He wants *you* to know that Jesus is the Son of God, so that *you* can have life, real life.

For Jews of those days, such as John, a father and a son were not two separate lives, but one ongoing life. A father hoped to live on in his son, and a son was a true son of his father if he continued his father's work, name and family. We think of the son–father relationship rather differently, so we have difficulty in seeing what John meant.

What he was saying was that if we look at Jesus and believe that he is the one *true* son of the Father, then we are saying that in Jesus we see what the Father is like. He is 'His Father all over again.' If we are to know what the 'Mind Behind the Universe' is like, we look at Jesus. In one sense we all are children of God, but only one was a true Son of God, the true likeness of the Father. But proud, snobbish, selfish people could not believe that this poor joiner from a hill village, who befriended the most peculiar people, could be a true demonstration of God. Least of all could they believe that the figure on the public gallows was showing us the Father's love.

But if you do believe that, then you begin to be able to *love* God. That love begins to spread out to other people. You know that you have begun a relationship with God which is eternal, and can never end. Jesus came, the Gospels were written and the church exists, so that *YOU* may have this life.

Introduction

We move on now to readings from the Book of Acts. It is a sort of second volume to St Luke's Gospel, and if you compare the opening verses of the Gospel and of Acts you will see this for yourself. They are obviously by the same man. We do not know what St Luke called the book, but the name 'Acts' has been attached to it.

Perhaps it would not have been called *The Acts of the Apostles* by Luke, but rather *The Acts of the Holy Spirit*. In his Gospel he had shown us the Spirit of God coming upon Mary, and the resulting Life of Jesus. In Acts he shows us the Spirit coming upon the church and the resulting life of the church. Luke was concerned to let us see that the same Spirit is at work among us, sinful mortals, as worked through Jesus of Nazareth. Quite wonderful things can happen through us if we open ourselves to God as Mary did at the beginning of Luke's Gospel, and as the disciples did at the beginning of Acts.

We sometimes get confused about all this, because some people have linked the idea of the Holy Spirit, the particular forms of highly emotional religion, with people being 'carried away', singing a particular type of hymn and so on. But while emotion does come into it, as it does in anything truly human, we must not allow modern 'labels' to come between us and what we read in the Bible.

Acts 1:1–5

'Acts' begins with a 'recap', to brush up your memory, and to link up with the Gospel.

In verse 4 some old versions of the Bible have 'eating with them'. Obviously the early church took it for granted that when Christians got together it was for *meals* and it was in *houses*. We take it for granted that it is for *service* and in *churches*. The early Christians would have been surprised to see what the church does today!

In verse 5 we see the summary of the Lord's instructions as to the next stage. John gives it more fully as he records what Jesus said at the Last Supper (John 14:15–21). The Lord promises 'the Comforter', if you are reading the AV, the 'Advocate', if it's the NEB. These are attempts to translate the word *parakletos*, which meant the man who stood by the accused in a trial, working for his release and acquittal, the 'prisoner's friend' it was called in army trials. So Jesus promises that something new will come into their lives: the Paraclete.

In the Gospels we saw the disciples watching Jesus, and occasionally helping him, but from now on they were to be spectators no longer. From that time onwards God was to be known as a power which worked through them, in them. God was to be known in the love which circulated through the church. It was no longer to be God-in-Jesus, but God-in-us.

We who are Jesus' followers today are not to be servants of some distant God, we are to be the ones through whom God's work will go on being done today. The work of rescuing the world is to be done through us. Christians should not say: 'Why doesn't God stop wars, heal the sick etc.?' God works through the people who have given themselves to Him because of what they have seen of His love in Jesus.

The Book of Acts begins the story. You are writing another chapter.

Acts 1:6–8

How incredibly stupid those disciples were! Fancy still asking if he was going to liberate Israel! Still thinking of the Kingdom of God in the traditional way! All Jesus' teaching, both before the Cross and after he had risen still does not seem to have sunk in.

We may be surprised at them and yet still people today are slow to move away from religious ideas they were taught as children, even though they are obviously outdated. People still cling to the hope that God is going to revive the old pattern eventually, and that the old buildings will be filled in the way we think they were one hundred years ago. Obviously that is not the way God works, but people still cling to it.

'It is not for you to know the dates and the time' said Jesus, and yet ever since his day there have been people who have been guessing at when he will return, or the end of the world will come. Down the centuries there have been groups who were sure that he would return on a certain date, and have even sold everything to be ready, and we still have them today. Jesus offers the Power of the Spirit in which his work can be carried on, and we have to go out to bear witness to his love, until the whole world knows how God loves us. We have to get on with the job, not make predictions about the future. Many Christians have become side-tracked into making predictions, and we must be clear that we are not going to be. It is important, then, that we avoid two mistakes:

(1) Thinking that God will turn the clock back and fulfil conventional hopes.

(2) Escaping from the hard work of loving all men in the Name of Jesus by getting caught up in predictions about the end of the world.

Acts 1:9 and Luke 24:50–53

Luke's Gospel ends in such a way that you would imagine that it was on Easter Sunday that Jesus parted from them. That story leaves us with a picture of Jesus blessing them with outstretched arms. The disciples understood from this that there were to be no more 'appearances', and yet they were filled with joy, which is not what they would have felt if they had seen Jesus leaving them.

In Acts, Luke corrects what might have been a wrong impression. He makes it clear that a long time elapsed between Easter and what we call 'the Ascension'. But it is the fuller account which bothers most modern people; the idea of Jesus taking off like a rocket seems ridiculous, so we have to try to get at what lies behind all this.

We have the picture of his being parted from them as he was in the act of blessing them. We see that it was something joyful, not really a parting. We see that they knew not to expect him to keep on coming back to them as he had been doing since he had risen. We see, as Matthew tells us clearly in Matt. 28:18, that they knew that Jesus is now the supreme authority in the universe: 'Lord of all being throned afar . . . yet to each loving heart how near!' as the hymn says. We see that their vision of Jesus from now on was, as St Paul put it, that he is 'filling the universe'; or, as the old negro spiritual put it: 'He's got the whole world in his hands!'

Perhaps that is how we can understand the experience these men had that day. The Jesus they had known as one of themselves, with hands scarred by human sin, filling the universe with his loving blessing. What they saw was not so much a figure disappearing into the blue, as Jesus becoming the Light behind all light, the Power behind all power, the Sun behind all suns . . . until it was too much for them, and went beyond their comprehension, and the vision clouded over. It is always hard to get words to express a great experience, so just think about it now yourself.

Acts 1:10–14

The 'two men in white' are back with us again! Call them angels if you want to. The disciples are left gaping at a blank where the face of Jesus had been, and the mysterious beings give them the assurance that he will be back one day. That, too is mysterious, and we have seen that there are dangers in pushing too far with trying to work out what it means.

Let us try to sum up the position: The disciples have been been given a world-mission to carry out. They have been told to wait until they receive the power with which to carry it out. They have been promised that Jesus is not finished with this world, and that some day a new chapter will be written. They have been told (Mark 13:33–7) that they must be like men who have been given a job to do while the foreman is out of the way. They must be ready for him to return at any minute. He expects to find them 'on the job'. That is more or less where our story has got us. Now it is a matter of waiting.

Luke's Gospel had begun with the promise of an angel to Mary that the Holy Spirit would come upon her; now the church is waiting for the promise of the Holy Spirit. They know after their behaviour when Jesus was arrested, that they could never do it in their own strength. In the light of the Cross they have had to face the truth about themselves, and they could never again trust themselves. Their mission could never be entrusted to people who were not aware of their own weakness and sin. There must be utter dependence on God. So now they gather together to wait, and it is interesting to notice that Jesus' brothers and mother are now part of the group who wait. The breach has been healed, it seems.

And for us? We too must seek the Power of His Spirit, not just as individuals, but as part of a group of followers.

Introduction

The great Jewish festive season ran from Passover for fifty days until Pentecost, a spring-harvest festival which was also observed as the celebration of the giving of the Ten Commandments. Pilgrims who had come a long way would stay up in the city for both festivals, while locals would go home after Passover and return for Pentecost. The city would be full once more.

But before we turn to the story, it would be a good thing to look back to something written in about 580 BC by Jeremiah, who lived in Jerusalem, and came through its destruction. There among the ruins he thought over what had gone wrong. He saw that good laws do not make people good. Even the Ten Commandments could not be kept by ordinary people. What was needed was not more laws, but a new spirit. Not something written on stone, but something deep down in the human heart. So you can read in Jeremiah 31:31 the message he passed on from God.

He foresaw that one day God would make a New Covenant. The Old Covenant (or Testament as we usually say) had been:

> Keep these commands and I will get you to the Promised Land, and prosper you.

That had lapsed because the people would not keep the commands, even when they signed in blood by means of sacrifice.

The New Covenant was to be a matter of *knowing* God deep down in your heart. If you know and love God, then you begin to want what He wants, and out of that 'new Spirit', a new relationship is born. Then, at the Last Supper, as we saw, Jesus spoke of the cup which he passed round as being this very New Covenant of which Jeremiah had spoken.

Now we are going to read of how, as the crowds gathered for Pentecost, the *Age of the Spirit* dawned.

Acts 2:1–3

Invisible power (wind)...a driving force...light and fire...a feeling of terrific power all round them, and within them...their words struggle to express what hit them that day. Whatever it was, it left them certain that the Power had been switched on, and the new life of the church had begun. Ordinary men and women now become the conductors of the same power which had been in Jesus.

Once more we must stress that this did not happen to them, and it will not happen to us, because they had reached some high level of goodness. In fact it was the very reverse. It happened to men and women who looked back on all that had happened leading up to the Cross, on all that had followed it, and realized how badly they had failed. Their own sin and weakness stood out so clearly in all of that. In contrast stood the Love of God which had called them, and had been patient with them through it all, and had finally entrusted them with His mission to the world, in spite of everything.

While it was necessary for *them* to have an experience which marked this new beginning clearly, it is not always necessary for us to have a similar one. John later on kept stressing in his letter that it is the experience of a new sort of love, within the family of those who confess the Christian Faith, which shows that The Holy Spirit has come upon us.

But every Christian group must pray urgently for a new outpouring of the Spirit, for only so can the Lord's work be done.

Acts 2:4–12

'Speaking in tongues' was obviously a very real thing in the early church, in fact sometimes it got out of hand, as we gather from what St Paul wrote to the Corinthian Church (I Cor. 14). In our own day there has been a rediscovery of it, and of course we have had the same problem that Paul had!

Our experience today has been of 'tongues' as a way of prayer rather than a missionary exercise. We do find cases of people speaking in languages which they could not possibly know, but it is seldom a way of communicating with people who only understand that language.

While this leaves many questions in our minds, we can see the main point: God was breaking out of the Hebrew setting for religion, beginning to reach out to all nations. Sadly it seems as if after the excitement of that day, the church fell back into thinking of itself as a Jewish movement, and the old nationalism crept back in. It took the great work of St Paul to lift it out of the rut, and to start spreading it in earnest among all nations, from about AD 50 onwards.

Yet speaking to people in their own language involves more than using the same words, as parents of teenage children will tell you! The Holy Spirit will give us understanding if we have learned to go out to people in love. Love always speaks for itself. It is pride and selfishness which build barriers and break down understanding. If we are really full of His Spirit of Love, there will be understanding.

K

Acts 2:12–24

Wouldn't it be wonderful if people thought us drunk as we came out of church? Imagine trying to explain to them that we were just 'happy' in God! God help us, we are much too sober!

So it is that Simon Peter speaks up, and after a bit of common-sense about it being too early in the morning for drunken orgies, he quotes the prophet Joel. He, like Jeremiah, had seen that one day there would be a new dawn, in which the Spirit would break out of the usual channels. The closed shop of the priesthood would be left behind. 'Tom, Dick and Harry' would become God's representatives. People you'd thought were 'just kids' would become men of vision. Old folk you'd thought were 'past it' would light up with new dreams, seeing new horizons, and even the poor down-trodden slaves would be rehumanized and become God's spokesmen. What a breakthrough!

That is what had happened, as Peter said. To our shame, we have to admit that over and over again we have tried to confine God to the 'official channels', and the Spirit has had the job of breaking out again.

In our day we see the Spirit breaking out in all sorts of ways. Wherever we look we see that people are forming groups of various sorts, to explore themselves, life or the universe. Down-trodden people, such as the Negroes in the Southern States of the USA have been rising up with a new dignity to assert that they *are* somebody. The Charismatic movement kindles life in all sorts of places, so that people who were brought up as Roman Catholics or as Protestants find a spiritual movement in which they can share, even in Northern Ireland. In our day too, new, disturbing winds of the Spirit are blowing, and it is an exciting time in which to live.

Acts 2:22–24, 37–41

What a change in Peter and his fellow disciples! Now he is standing up, challenging the whole nation. The man who had denied his Lord now flings down the challenge fearlessly. The working man who had never been to a theological college preaches a sermon which is still ringing through history. That is the biggest miracle yet, and if it had not been for the miracle that happened to those men and women, we would never have heard of Jesus of Nazareth.

(In case you wonder about how that sermon was recorded, it is worth noting that missionaries today have the experience of going to a village and finding that people can repeat word for word the sermon they preached there years before. We lost that power when we gained the printed word.)

We have to bring it home to twentieth-century man that it is over him that God agonizes, and that what went for the people of Jerusalem in AD 30 goes for the people of Edinburgh, London, Moscow today.

If they ask what they can do about it, the answer is the same as the one Peter gave: Be ready to change your way of life, turn to God and be baptized into His Family, and you will receive the gift of the Holy Spirit too. It will make a new man of you! Or woman! The Spirit is not for apostles only, it is for the world, and the task of spreading the Gospel is not for priests, ministers or clergy alone, but for people like fishermen, joiners and their wives and mothers.

The Love of God is to reach out in ever-widening circles down the centuries, until it reaches you and me, and then as we open our lives to Him, it goes on flowing through us, out into the world, down into the future. Nobody who receives good news can keep it to himself, and that is why it goes on being passed on. How are you going to pass it on?

Introduction

We have grown up with the idea that the church is a massive, state-backed institution, very much part of 'the establishment'! In some places the clergy are state officials, and many ordinary people think of the church along with the schools and the police as a way of keeping people in order. That is why they do not want to go to church, and would not dream of going to the church for spiritual help. That is why one hears all sorts of people saying that they can be Christian without going to church.

But this week we are going to look at what this word *church* really means. The picture which emerges is not a bit like the picture of the church which most people have in mind.

It is quite true that you can be a respectable citizen without singing hymns and listening to a sermon each Sunday morning. It is quite true that many who do go to church do not seem to be very Christian. But perhaps that is not what the church really is. If we really get down to brass tacks in our thinking about the church, then perhaps we will come up with some new answers.

Acts 2:42–47

This is a picture of the church as it is meant to be. Look through the passage carefully, and pick out the features that should be seen in the life of any congregation.

Notice that the effect of the Holy Spirit upon them was not just that they spoke in tongues, but that they began to have a whole new way of life based on 'sharing'.

In those days poverty was real and deadly, and it was remarkable for them that when they shared, poverty disappeared and there was plenty to go round, and to spare. This real sharing has shrunk down to putting a few coppers in the plate, which is a shame. There have always been groups who have tried to share life completely. Monks and nuns have. Various communities throughout the ages, including many today, have tried it with whole families. The Iona Community tried to work out an 'economic discipline' (see *The Household of Faith* by Ralph Morton), and in many ways we have kept on working at it, but it is not easy in our complex society today.

The basic question is: If this passage shows us the blue-print the Spirit is working on, are we going to co-operate? Would we be glad to be moved in this direction? Are we looking for a life-sharing like this? Don't just ask *yourself* these questions, share your questioning with others. Open yourselves to the Spirit together, so that He can get to work in you and through you.

Acts 3:1–10

Yesterday we read that 'signs and wonders' were performed through the apostles, and today's reading gives us an example. We see Peter and John doing the sort of thing that Jesus used to do. As Jesus said in the words recorded in John 14: 'The works that I do, shall you do also. . . .'

There is a story that some visitors were being shown round the Vatican and its treasures, long ago. The Pope, who claimed to be Peter's successor, commented 'Peter's successor no longer needs to say "Gold and silver have I none"'. The visitor replied: 'But neither can you say "In the Name of Jesus, get up and walk."' That is not just a story against popes, it goes for any church. As the church gained earthly power, it lost spiritual power. Strangely, now that the church is losing earthly power, there are signs all over the world that it is gaining spiritual power again.

Thanks to advances in medical healing, a lot of superstition has been cleared out, and this was much needed. There was a tendency to confuse spiritual healing with using the name of Jesus as a sort of magic charm. Perhaps that is why the river of healing went underground for centuries, although it has never been lost sight of completely.

In our own day many doctors are realizing that medical healing does not have all the answers, and that the trouble with many patients cannot be dealt with by pills or by surgery. We begin to see a new place for spiritual healing. Cameron Peddie carried on a healing ministry in the Gorbals, Glasgow, and his book *The Forgotten Talent* is now a classic. In *Healing & Christianity* Morton Kelsey traces the story of Christian healing, and its current developments in a fuller, more theological way. There are many others too, some of them become 'cranky', and one has to be careful about reading in this area. 'Healing' has become big business in the USA, and many people have been put off.

Acts 3:11–16

Peter loses no time in making it plain that he and John are not 'holy men' or 'healers'. He knew that he, and his fellow disciples had made a mess of things, so he comes straight to the point. It is Jesus who is working through them, and he goes on to punch home the message of the Cross and the Resurrection.

Somebody once said that it is our job as Christians to point to Jesus and then to get out of the light! Jesus himself once said: 'You are the light of the world... let your light so shine before men that they may see your good work and glorify your Father in Heaven'. That is our calling: to do good in such a way that people do not notice us, but are brought to glorify God. There are ways of doing good that draw attention to the do-gooder. There is a satisfaction in having a reputation as a good man, or as a healer. But if our 'light' advertises ourselves, then we have failed.

So Peter points to Jesus. He speaks plainly, not using the Jewish preaching style. He uses his own words, or should we say that the Spirit inspired him to speak in this down to earth way? We must not be held back because we feel that we cannot use churchy language. There is nothing particularly Christian about language that sounds 'old-fashioned', or even about language that sounds like the latest American religious phraseology. The Gospel is best expressed in the words that come naturally. The Spirit speaks through the real 'us', not through somebody else's way of putting it.

You can begin by sharing your own experience with others, and letting the Holy Spirit guide you from there. But the Christian who does not try to spread the Good News soon slips back. You may not consider it a good idea to go around asking people if they are saved, but you must find your own way of spreading the Gospel.

Acts 4:1–24

This is a long story, but worth reading as a whole. In verse 13 we read that to the priests these two were untrained laymen. Yet the trained professionals were at a loss to know what to make of them.

We still have professionals, calling them ministers or priests, but it ill befits those who follow in the steps of those first untrained laymen to create a new class of professional religious men who make the laymen feel like second-class religious citizens.

One often hears people suggesting that the layman's job is to help the minister, as if the minister is the important person, and the people of the congregation are just hangers-on and helpers. In fact it is the other way round. The word *lay* really means *the people*, and the professional is only there in order to help Christians to be the People of God. It is the men and the women in the fellowship of the church who are really doing the Christian work, where they live and work. The professionals are only there to support them.

In verse 19 we have Peter's great reply, echoed by many people down the ages. For instance when Luther was being tried, he said: 'Here I stand, I cannot do otherwise.' Martin Luther King, leading the Negro rights campaign threw away his gun saying: 'The quality, not the longevity of one's life is what is important. If you are cut down in a movement that is designed to save the soul of a nation, then no other death could be more redemptive.' And he was cut down.

To obey God rather than men is always costly. Peter found the spirit to do it, or rather the Holy Spirit found Peter and enabled him to do it. It was not that Peter was brave, but that the Spirit gave him courage. You too may be naturally timid or shy, but the Spirit will give you courage when you need it.

Look up the hymn: 'I'm not ashamed to own my Lord....'

Introduction

In about AD 53 one of Jesus' leading followers, called Paul, wrote a letter to a little group of Christians in the city of Corinth, in Greece. It was a city famed for its immorality, a centre of trade, and an important place. In Acts 18 we read of how the church there began, in a room next-door to the Jewish synagogue.

As we read this letter, we cannot but be struck by the way in which the church had come down a long way from the ideal picture we studied last week. Paul in this letter is facing the problems which beset the church. With some he deals gently, and with some he deals sternly. When he wrote this letter, or series of letters, he had no idea that one day it would be included in Holy Scripture. It bears all the marks of a letter written under pressure to people with real problems. At times as we read it, we see Paul as a man of his times, very conscious that he was not easy to get on with, and liable to pride. But through this very human person, dealing with very human problems, we see the Spirit at work, often raising him to sublime heights. So remember that we are not concerned with good people, but with sinners like Paul, through whom the Love of God can work. People miss the point when they point out that Paul was far from perfect. The message is that God's Love can work through people who have real faults, like Paul, the Corinthians, you and me.

L

I Corinthians 1: 10–24

From this letter we gather that already divisions were appearing. Different church leaders had slightly different angles on things. You can see this clearly if you read the New Testament. Instead of seeing this variety as an enrichment, people were tending to line up behind their favourites, and factions were appearing. Each faction was saying: 'Our view is the right one.'

The leaders in question were Cephas, which is just the Aramaic word for a rock, so in its Latin form it is 'Peter', our old friend Simon Peter. The other is Apollos, and he is one of the mystery-men of the Bible, obviously a leading figure, but we do not know much about him. Some backed Paul, while some just claimed to be Christ's men. Paul is horrified at this sort of division among those who are called by Jesus to love one another. Had not Jesus said that it is by our love for each other that men will know that we are his disciples? So no Christian is right while he is divided from his fellow-Christian by some argument.

We live in a day in which Christians are increasingly feeling that our divisions are a scandal. Naturally there are differences, and nobody really wants all Christians to worship and think in the same way. *Unity but not uniformity* is the slogan today. We have a lot to learn from Paul here. He heads straight for the Cross. Our divisions come because we try to be too damnably clever. At the heart of things is the mystery no words can ever describe, no theory or theology can cover the whole mystery. It can only be expressed by a man on a gallows, rising from the dead.

When we find ourselves arguing, we should learn the lesson Paul taught. We should together 'survey the wondrous Cross', knowing that what unites us is greater than all the differences. Let us all share with each other how we see things, and appreciate the different angles on the Gospel. But let our oneness in Christ be the overwhelming theme of our common worship.

I Corinthians 6: 12–20

Paul seemed very permissive to the people of his day. The Jews had grown up to think of religion as a system of rules and taboos, but Paul taught that it was more a matter of love, and of faith. It seems that at Corinth there were some people who were saying: 'Paul says I can do anything...whoopee!' The passage we read is Paul's answer to this.

He quotes a local saying about food being for the stomach, and it refers to the fact that food, drink and prostitutes were all openly available on the local market, and the attitude was that if you had a stomach, then feed it, etc. We have come across the attitude today. Paul tries to lift the whole thing on to a higher plane. He does not just take a negative line, saying: 'Thou shalt not....' He tries to let them see that the body, and all its organs are something wonderful, something which can be a Temple for the Holy Spirit. We might say that it is a 'transistor' which can be tuned in to God.

Our physical activities, especially sex, all have spiritual overtones. If you miss these, then you miss the secret of living. The person who allows his life to be dominated by the physical appetites soon becomes degraded by them. And we in our 'permissive society'? It is no use our just taking a negative line. Christians who are against everything, and who only speak up when they are opposing something a lot of other people enjoy, get the faith a bad name. We have to be positive. Christ-filled lives, radiating love and understanding, in which the body is enjoyed but not over-indulged, these are the best advertisements for the faith. In the long run the people who have gone all-out for 'enjoyment' find themselves envying the person with a serene and balanced life. We should be the people who know best how to enjoy food, drink and sex, and how to live satisfied lives even if we have to deny ourselves.

Spend time thinking of your body, see it as the Temple of the Holy Spirit, a Godly Transistor.

I Corinthians 12:4–13

Actually, it is worth reading the whole chapter! We use the word 'member' quite freely, forgetting where it started: here. We have 'members' of the Miners' Club, of the pigeon-racing club and so on. But the word began by meaning a part of the body, and the NEB translates it 'limb or organ'. The Christian community was seen as the Body of Christ with each member being a 'limb or organ'. Through that Body God's Spirit flows, giving to the parts of the Body the power to do the work of Jesus. People who belong to that Body find that spread through the group are different 'gifts', the gift of healing, of speaking in God's Name (prophecy=being a spokesman), tongues, and so on.

The church, then, is not just another organization. It is the flesh and blood through which Christ's work goes on. Sometimes the so-called church slips into being just one organization among many, but then it is no longer truly the church.

Our calling is to represent Jesus by the Power of the Spirit. All that Jesus was, is present in the church by the Power of the Holy Spirit, and our priority is that week by week we should offer our bodies to Him as a living sacrifice (Romans 12:1), so that he can use us to continue His Work in the world today. The more we give ourselves to Him, the more powerfully the Spirit can work through us.

Paul's problem was that in this church, as in some today, people who were manifesting some particular Gift of the Spirit were carried away by their pride. Perhaps the healers wanted to make it a healing mission, and the prophets wanted everybody to sit around listening to them and so on. Without the Gifts of the Spirit the church becomes just another human organization, but temptations beset even the most Spirit-filled church. This is a very important chapter.

I Corinthians 13

This chapter is one of the best known in the Bible. Many who would not call themselves Christian, acknowledge it as one of the greatest things ever written. Yet it is often forgotten that it arose out of Paul's struggle to deal with sordid one-upmanship in a group of Christians. He stresses the superiority of Love over all the other things he has been speaking about.

The phrase about the mirror in verse 12 needs a word of explanation. Mirrors in Paul's day were made of metal. Those who can remember trying to shave in the metal mirrors during the war know how difficult it is to see properly in a metal mirror. You adjust it so that one bit of your face is in focus, but the rest becomes a blur. It is hard to get the over-all picture. That is a wonderful illustration of how we see life. Thank God for the assurance that when we have grown fully mature in love, we shall be able to see the whole picture, and to *know*.

Read the chapter slowly, and let it show you where you need to grow. The last verse of chapter 12 and the first verse of chapter 14 really belong to the chapter we have read; it is a pity that they were cut off. They make it clear that Paul is offering this as the Christian's ambition. We are not making our aim in life to be one up on the Joneses, but we are aiming at being utterly loving. Even wanting to be a great preacher or healer is not a truly Christian ambition. The only true aim is to become a loving person. That is the aim which takes us beyond this world altogether, into eternal life. Is that your ambition?

WEEK 30 LOOKING FORWARD TO SEEING HIM

Introduction

Our final four readings take us back to the Last Supper. St John gives us five chapters of profound sayings by Jesus at the Last Supper. You can spend a life-time pondering these words, and still find new things in them. It is to these that we turn as an end to this study. Jesus looks forward to the future in these chapters, and you too must look forward. You must decide 'Where do I go from here?'

If you just close the book and go back to living as you did before, then you will lose anything you have gained. Nothing is sadder than the person who has studied the Life of Jesus, and who stops there saying 'I know all that.' It is rather like the person who has stopped a course of penicillin midway, and then, when they catch an infection which is dangerous, they find that penicillin will no longer work for them.

As a follow-up you must find people with whom to share, if you are not already doing so, and we will be thinking about this on Day 3. There are other ways of following it up. You can explore one specific book in the Bible, by getting what we call a 'commentary'. This is a book which goes over one particular part of the Bible verse by verse. William Barclay's are well known, but there are many others. Some are 'conservative' and some are 'radical', which is what you would expect with human beings. The conservatives take a very strict line as to what they think you must believe if you are to be a Christian, while the radicals question everything. If you have not been warned, you can be upset by either of the extremes. But you can pursue your way, learning from both, but carried away by neither. Just go on exploring, trusting the Holy Spirit to guide you, and you will find that new truths are continually dawning on you. Sometimes you will come to the 'spiritual deserts' when it all seems dry and dull, but if you keep pushing on, you will come out again into 'green pastures'.

John 14: 1–6

These are some of the best loved words in the Bible. In
them Jesus seeks to re-assure his friends, past and present,
about the future, drawing illustrations from travelling in
the Middle East.

If you ask the way across some stretch of desert and
mountain, you will not be shown a road, you will be
introduced to a man who has crossed it frequently, and
who knows its dangers and its resting-places. As the party
sets out, a scout goes on ahead to check the way, and to
prepare the resting-place for that night. He comes back
and leads the party on to the place he has prepared. That
is how we are to reach Our Father's Home, says Jesus. He
himself is the true and living Way, and he will get us
home. It seems that Thomas wanted some more specific
instructions on the future, and don't we all? But Jesus
insists that The Way is to trust him and to let him guide
us. We do not need fortune-telling or astrology to predict
the future. He has gone on into tomorrow, so the way and
the next resting-place are ready for us.

These words came at a time when the disciples had
everything to worry about, from a human point of view,
and they were going to be completely shattered (see the
last verses of the previous chapter). Yet in the face of all
this, Jesus reassures them. That is why we as Christian
people can be forward looking, without being shallow
optimists. We do not need to pretend that tragedies,
atrocities and personal defeats never happen. They do, but
Our Lord leads us through them.

We usually read these words at funerals, and death *is*
one of the stages on the journey, but this passage applies to
far more than that particular stage.

If we walk in his Way,

trust in his Truth

and live his Life

then we have nothing to fear in the future, and the rest of
life is a journey Home, so that we can travel on in hope.

John 14: 7–20

'Have I been all this time with you and do you still not know me?' How often Jesus must say this to us too! As Thomas had looked for the wrong sort of answer to his questions about the future (v. 5), so now Philip is looking for the wrong sort of revelation of God. The experiences they had been through with the Joiner from Nazareth had been wonderful in their own way, but surely there was something more to God than that? There was, but not what Philip was expecting, as he would find the next day.

The way to know God is here, right beneath our noses, while people look in all sorts of exotic places, or else give up altogether. We sit round a table, share bread and wine perhaps, focus on Jesus and give ourselves to carrying on his work, acting as his representatives. As his representatives? That is what 'in my name' means in verse 14 and in other places. It does not mean that you tack 'for Jesus sake, Amen.' at the end of *your* prayer. It means: when you are acting in your capacity as his 'rep', then you can know God, not just as the Power of Love over us, but also as the Power of Love within us ... the Holy Spirit.

Our journey into the future does not mean becoming religious in some strange way; it just means getting on with life, sharing it with Jesus in the fellowship of His People. It is in doing His work in the every-day things of life that we grow to know him, and there is a real danger in seeking special religious experiences. Our prayer and worship are not to be escapes into another world, but they should light up our work, our joys, our sorrows, our loves, and all the trivial things of life with a new, glory. These are the 'teaching materials' in the school of life, and as we work with them we come to *know* God.

John 15:1–14

A vine is to be seen in most houses in the Mediterranean area, climbing up the wall, spreading its network of branches over the buildings, and often trained to make a shady corner in the courtyard. That is the picture which Jesus leaves us of our life together as Christian people. The inter-twining of branches is his illustration of that love for each other which is to be the hall-mark of the true church. Our lives are to be inter-woven so that we all support one another.

Being a Christian is not only something you must do on your own. Of course there are depths which we must explore in privacy, but that is not the whole story. The Christian life is like football, in that it is something people do together. If you are to grow on from here, you must find people with whom to share your faith and life. That is not always easy. Many churches have very little of this life-sharing. People in church often sit separated by yards of timber as if they were afraid of getting involved with each other. We have to find people with whom to share at depth, and this may often mean searching it out.

You may find such a Christian fellowship in a local congregation, but if not, then like many Christians you may find this in movements that are not actually local congregations. There are many centres of Christian life which have movements associated with them in which people can find prayer and Bible Study together. One can think, for instance of Iona (The Abbey, Iona, Argyll) or the Community, Taize, France, or of the monasteries connected with either the Roman Catholic Church or the Church of England. The people who go to these centres often meet in their own localities for mutual support. The Scripture Union has an office in each of the main cities and there are often Bible Study Groups connected with them. 'Seek and you shall find' as Jesus said.

John 17: 1–5 and 20–26

On the brink of the awful experience which was to begin
in an hour or two's time, Jesus gives Glory to God. That is
positive thinking at its most sublime. It is one thing to
glorify God when all goes well, but when you are awaiting
something which makes you 'sweat blood' it is a different
question. There will be times when The Way leads us
through experiences that are nightmarish, but then, like
Jesus, it is all the more important not to let the darkness
get us down, but to lift up our hearts in praise. Praise is
one of the greatest weapons in our armoury for the battle
against evil.

Remember that the 'glory' he speaks of is the glory of
love, not the glory of 'I'm the greatest'. Love's glory is in
how low it will stoop, how much it will bear, how
completely self can be forgotten for love of others. We have
a natural hunger for 'glory' and the world tries to satisfy it
in many ways, but we must seek the true glory.

As Jesus moves on to pray for those of us who will follow
him later, note that he prays that we may be 'one'. He
does not pray that we shall be good or kind, or even
that the churches shall be full every Sunday! He prays that
his followers may be united in love, and well he may pray
that with urgency! We have much need of that prayer!
Often it is the most religious, and those who speak most
about being Christian, who are the most divisive. If only
Christians were as concerned to build up this one-ness as
their Lord is, how different history would be!

How can the world believe the Gospel of love unless it
sees that network of Love (v. 21)? And we cannot come to
heaven, where he is, unless we grow in one-ness with
others (v. 24). If we are truly growing to know Jesus, then
we will have an ever-deepening one-ness with an ever-
widening circle of people, until we come to the complete
one-ness of Love 'where He is'.

This book is meant to be a beginning, not an ending, so its end is a beginning!

As St John said in his Gospel:

> This book is written so that you may hold
> the faith that Jesus is the Christ, the
> Son of God; and that through
> this faith you may possess life by His Name.

May you keep on growing in the knowledge of Jesus
until, beyond this world altogether
you come to know as you are known
and see Him face to face,
made like Him.

INDEX OF REFERENCES

INDEX OF REFERENCES